My First Forty Cars

My First Forty Cars

An Automotive Memoir

NELSON BOLAN

McFarland & Company, Inc., Publishers
Jefferson, North Carolina, and London

Library of Congress Cataloguing-in-Publication Data

Bolan, Nelson.
    My first forty cars : an automotive memoir / Nelson Bolan.
        p.   cm.
    Includes index.

    ISBN 0-7864-1624-6 (softcover : 50# alkaline paper)

    1. Bolan, Nelson—Anecdotes.   2. Automobiles—United
States—Anecdotes.   3. Automobile drivers—United States
—Anecdotes.   4. Automobiles—Collectors and collecting—
Anecdotes.   I. Title.
TL140.B495A3   2003
629.28'3'092—dc22   2003014376

British Library cataloguing data are available

Manufactured in the United States of America

On the cover: The author's 1917 Dodge Brothers, 1951 DeSoto Club Coupe,
1938 Chrysler and 1962 Buick LeSabre convertible

McFarland & Company, Inc., Publishers
  Box 611, Jefferson, North Carolina 28640
    www.mcfarlandpub.com

Contents

Introduction

It has been over fifty years since car number one. Lots of rubber has met the road and lots of gears have been shifted since then.

Most of us don't especially plan to buy specific automobiles most of the time. Rather we adapt what is available in our price range to our needs or desires at the time of purchase. Out of economic necessity I had to learn to do many repairs myself, making my share of mistakes in the process. Fortunately, none of my mistakes posed a danger to me or to anyone else. As time passed I became more bold and tackled more complicated tasks.

Although I have never had a foreign car (because I have no interest in them), I have had a few Rolls Kinardly and a few Runzonly. For the uninitiated, a Rolls Kinardly rolls downhill fine but can hardly go uphill at all. A Runzonly runs only when you push it.

Of my four grandparents only my mother's father knew how to drive an automobile. I do not know when or why or how he learned to drive, but he became the chauffeur for a wealthy family in 1910 and drove for them until he retired in the mid-1930s. From 1900 until 1910 he drove a horse car; what we now refer to as a streetcar or trolley car was drawn by horses on tracks prior to being converted to electric power. My mother got her first full-time job as the secretary to the service manager of a Pierce-Arrow dealer in 1919 and worked there until 1923, when the dealership went out of business. While no one ever mentioned this to me, I strongly suspect that my grandfather was instrumental in my mother's getting that job. It was not considered necessary for a girl to graduate from high school in those days, and my grandparents could not afford the luxury of high school for her, so she paid her own way, working after school and on Saturdays and during

1

The author's grandfather and his wealthy employer's 1921 Pierce-Arrow seven-passenger touring car. The picture was taken in 1923 in Cape Cod, where the employer's
family spent the summer. The author's grandfather was the chauffeur for the family for twenty-five years, until he retired. Pierce-Arrow used right-hand drive until
the 1923 models.

summer vacations. All my mother's sisters also worked their way
through high school.

The two brothers in the family became interested in automobiles,
and one of them spent his adult life working for General Motors. My
grandfather told the story of one of my uncles, who put an engine back
together and neglected to put the cotter pins in through the castle nuts
on the connecting rods. The resulting clatter from the engine a few
miles later reminded him. Besides getting quite a ribbing from my
grandfather and others, he had to get the car towed back home, then
do the job right the next time.

After the Pierce-Arrow dealership closed in 1923, my mother's
next job was in the main office of the local AAA. It was there that she
met my father, a member of AAA. To my father, an automobile was a
way of getting from point A to point B, nothing else. During his Model
T Ford days my father got into the habit of buying five gallons of gasoline each time he bought gas, which filled half a tank on a Model T.
That would always get him through the week until the next payday. For

the rest of his life he bought gas only five gallons at a time, no matter which car he owned at the time.

My mother did not learn to drive until the family bought a 1932 Chevrolet coach (two-door sedan) and she had two preschool children. The apartment we lived in was owned by a kindly retired couple. Mr. Hayes had been a Packard salesman, and one of his duties was to teach people how to drive them. Mrs. Hayes would look after us two small children while Mr. Hayes took my mother out for a driving lesson in his gray 1927 Packard sedan with a rear-mounted disc wheel spare tire. Eventually, they went out in the 1932 Chevrolet coach in the evenings and on Saturdays when my father was home. When she was experienced and confident enough, the family would ride with my father to his office, then my mother would have the car all day until it was time to pick up my father from his office around 5:30 P.M.

So far I have just mentioned my mother's side of the family. While my father had no interest in cars, one of his brothers, my uncle Joe, had enough for both of them. My paternal grandfather was a contractor who built streets, homes, and other buildings and had a lot of gasoline-powered equipment, but he never learned to drive an automobile. During the 1920s he owned a Franklin. When the time came to sell it he advertised it in the Sunday newspaper. One of the unique features of every Franklin of that era was its extremely smooth-riding spring system. My grandfather told all those who called to inquire about the car that "it rides like a baby buggy."

While this book covers cars I owned, there were a few other cars in my life before I was old enough to drive or own a car that I will mention briefly. One was a 1928 Cadillac owned by my maternal grandfather. It was a Brewster green four-door sedan with black fenders and aprons. It had a light on the front of each rear fender that would go on whenever the door next to it was opened, illuminating the running board. My grandfather had driven this car since it was new; when his employer passed away, it was willed to my grandfather. I remember riding in it many times as a child. In 1937 he traded this car for a 1937 Dodge, a green four-door sedan with a built-in trunk. He drove this car for six or seven years, and when his health began to deteriorate, his grown children took over most of the driving duties. Eventually he gave up driving and signed the car over to one of his children, who usually drove him around.

Another car was in my life only briefly but was very important to

The author's grandfather and his employer's 1911 Packard. Whoever took the picture did not get it centered exactly, missing the dual spare tires on the rear end. The
vertical tubular object at the very rear is an accessory gas-filled shock absorber. The
other rear spring would also have had one. The license plate is mounted very high,
above the shock absorber. Many cars of this era were like this one, where the rear
fender extended out parallel to the road. It was mistakenly thought that this would
keep dust and so forth from getting into the rear passenger compartment. The shiny
object between the door and front fender is the "ooga" horn.

me at the time. Owned by the local AAA affiliate, it was a 1942 Pontiac, on which I learned to drive in 1944. It was a maroon four-door
sedan, preblackout, with "student driver" on each side as well as on the
trunk. It also had a red flag on the corner of each bumper. Even though
it was used strictly by students, it wasn't too bad although it would
have been considered rather rough for a family car almost three years
old. Inside, the right front floor had an accelerator pedal and a brake
pedal for the instructor. Because my driving lessons took place during
World War II my instructor was a woman. She did her job very well,
and I passed my test to get a permanent driver's license on the first try.

The other car that influenced my early driving life was the family
1940 Oldsmobile. It was the lowest-priced two-door sedan (the "60"
series) made by Oldsmobile that year. It cost $888.00; only the "60"
series coupe was cheaper. The only accessory was the heater/defroster
package. The 60 series had a six-cylinder engine. This car was medium

This is probably the first car the author ever rode in. It was the family car at the time. It appears to be a 1923 or 1924 Model T Ford roadster. The lad in the driver's seat is the author's older brother, age about eighteen months. In the shadow is the author's father. The shadow of the author's mother, who took the picture, can be seen cast over the left rear fender and wheel.

gray; my parents bought it about a month before the 1941 models appeared in the showrooms. The six-cylinder models were not available with Hydra-Matic in 1940, but my father would not have bought a Hydra-Matic-equipped car anyway.

For two years, from mid-1944 until mid-1946, this was the only car available to me to drive. With four drivers in the family it was not mine to use exclusively.

Although I do not remember it, the family car when I was born was a Model T Ford. In September 1930 my parents traded it for a used 1930 Ford Tudor (two-door sedan), built in April 1930. Later on, they traded that in for a new 1932 Chevrolet Coach (two-door sedan). This is the oldest car I can remember; it was maroon with black fenders and aprons. This was later traded in on a new 1935 Chevrolet Master Coach with knee action but no trunk. It had a radio, a heater, a defroster and, of course, "suicide" doors opening at the front. My father said that this car didn't run right and took it back to the dealer several times, but to no avail. The salesman who had sold him the car said he had looked

PHONE CANAL 7480

THE BAUER AUTO SALES CO.

Ford

316-322 E. SIXTH ST.   CINCINNATI, O.

Mr. Nelson   Bolan   Sept. 16, 1930
3824 Woodburn Ave.,   Motor #3213461
City

TERMS: STRICTLY NET, NO CASH DISCOUNT ALLOWED   WE CARRY THE LARGEST STOCK OF PARTS IN THE CITY

1	Used Ford model A Tudor sedan		375	00
		All. used car $25.00		
		Cash deposit 75.00		
			100	00
			275	00

PAID
SEP 17 1930
THE BAUER AUTO SALES CO
PER

Howard

up the serial number and learned that the car was partly completed during a strike. Exactly what "partly completed" meant, he didn't say. Whether he actually did what he said, I don't know, but my father accepted the story. The salesman knew how disappointed my father was with the car and let him trade it for a 1936 Master Coach a year later. This model sported knee action and exactly the same equipment (again with no trunk) but no suicide doors. The 1936 model was kept until December 1938, when it was traded in on a new, blue 1939 Oldsmobile (60 series) two-door sedan. A year later that car was traded in on the 1940 Oldsmobile mentioned earlier.

My father's brother, my uncle Joe, was always doing something on a car, and his mechanical knowledge was extensive. There were four sons and a daughter in that family. Uncle Joe's sister married in 1920, and in the winter of 1921–1922 her first baby was due. She and her husband lived about two miles away, and her husband would drop her off at her family's home on his way to work as someone was always there in case she needed help. Then he would pick her up on his way home from work. Uncle Joe had a Dort automobile and was still living at home at this time. (Mr. Dort had been a partner of William C. Durant when Durant founded General Motors in 1908.)

One particular winter day was raw and bitter and freezing cold, and Uncle Joe's Dort had been parked outside all day. Suddenly his sister realized that her baby would be arriving very soon. Someone called her husband at work and told him to go straight to the hospital and they would meet him there. Meanwhile, Uncle Joe went to get the Dort started and bring it closer to the steps so his sister and their mother could get into the car easier. On his way out of the house Uncle Joe grabbed a section of newspaper and rolled it up as he walked to the car. He then opened up the Dort's hood, set the end of the rolled-up newspaper on fire, shoved the burning newspaper underneath the Dort's updraft carburetor and held it there about ten seconds. Other family members were about to have heart failure wondering why Uncle Joe had picked such a time to set the car on fire. But Uncle Joe knew what he was doing! He removed the burning newspaper, stomped it out on

Opposite, top: The author, age ten, in front of the family's 1939 Oldsmobile. An aunt's 1934 Chevrolet rumble seat coupe is parked in the background.

   Bottom: Invoice for my father's purchase of the used 1930 Ford Model A on September 16, 1930. The $25.00 allowance on the used car was for the Model T Roadster shown on page 5.

the ground, closed the hood and got into the driver's seat. The engine started right up as soon as Uncle Joe turned on the ignition and just touched the starter switch.

What Uncle Joe had done was heat the carburetor and the intake manifold to vaporize all the gasoline in the entire intake system so that the engine would start instantly without his having to use the choke and risk flooding the engine at such a crucial time.

The story had a happy ending. Thanks to Uncle Joe's safe driving and the Dort's dependable performance, they arrived at the hospital in plenty of time, and a beautiful, healthy baby was born with no complications.

With such a background, perhaps it is not surprising that I developed a lifelong fascination with the automobile. Certainly I have owned my share. The cars are listed in the order in which I acquired them. From the mid-1940s until the mid-1980s I often had at least two cars at one time. Only a couple were "parts cars." None of the cars was purchased new by me; the newest one was at least four years old. Three were given to me, and you can imagine what kind of shape they were in. Six came from original owners, including one who had owned the car for twenty-five years. All were passenger cars. All were built in the United States except a full-size Dodge van station wagon, assembled in Canada to U.S. specifications (all Dodge vans were assembled there at that time). All were regular "bread and butter" cars; none was a classic; none was customized. All of them had the standard OEM wheels, which were disc since the mid-1930s. One had demountable rims on disc wheels, four had demountable rims on wooden wheels, and one had locking rings on disc wheels (the spare was a complete wheel and tire assembly). Tire sizes included 13, 14, 15, 16, 17, 19, 20, 23 and 25 inch varieties. One car had a rear-opening hood; twenty-one had front-opening hoods; and sixteen had side-opening hoods.

1 · 1929 Chevrolet

Since I acquired my first car before I was twenty-one years old, my father insisted that the title and insurance be in his name. I knew that I could not legally buy or sell a car until I turned twenty-one so I readily agreed. He proposed to pay the insurance premium himself, to ensure that it was indeed paid, and I would pay him my share. This car was added to the family car policy as a second car to the 1940 Oldsmobile 60.

In the summer of 1946 my older brother was discharged from military service, and I graduated from high school a few weeks before my eighteenth birthday. My brother was one of the last people to be drafted in World War II, and I was one of the first eighteen-year-olds not to be called up for the draft. In celebration of my brother's safe return, my graduation from high school, and my not having to go into the military, our parents decided that we were ready for the responsibility of automobile ownership. A friend of theirs had a 1929 Chevrolet Coach (Fisher Body's name for a two-door sedan), but he seldom drove it because he lived in a nice neighborhood about a block beyond the end of a streetcar line. The place where he worked was on the same streetcar line about half-hour's ride from home. His family and friends knew that he didn't like to drive, and they all accepted that fact. The price he and my parents agreed upon was $100.00. I was eighteen years old and the car was seventeen years old. My parents' friend had purchased the car in 1937 from its original owner, a fellow he had worked with, after the original owner agreed to have the car painted as part of the deal.

By this time Uncle Joe and Uncle John both worked for the same company. Uncle John was an executive, and Uncle Joe held a position of

responsibility over the company's fleet of cars and trucks. Since my father had no mechanical knowledge or interest and neither did the man from whom the car was purchased, my father prevailed upon his two brothers to look the car over and see whether any repairs were needed. Until my father, my brother and I went to the friend's house to get the car and saw it in his garage, none of us had seen it. Because neither my brother nor I had experience with mechanical brakes, my father insisted on driving the car to his brothers' company's garage, about twenty miles away. That was the one and only time my father drove that car or was even inside it.

Top: The author, age nineteen, is at the far left. The author's parents are standing near him on the back porch.
  Bottom: Rear view of car number one, the 1929 Chevrolet.

Uncle Joe had come a long way since the unique way of warming up his Dort some twenty-five years earlier. He pronounced that the car's valves needed to be ground. The company mechanic worked on it in his spare time, so about ten days elapsed before we were finally able to get the car.

Two of the tires were worn recaps that needed to be replaced. While the valves were being ground my father and I located two new 6.00 × 20 Goodyear tires. The car's original tires were a size 4.50 × 20, but we could not find any that size, and 6.00 × 20 was the next over-size. He located one and I located the other at different tire dealers. Since both were Goodyear, they had matching diamond tread. The new tires were wider than the other. So they were put on the rear, and the good 4.50s were put on the front for easier steering.

Just a couple of weeks after my brother and I began using the car, a tooth broke off of low gear. Back to the uncles' place. They removed the transmission, took it apart and gave us the broken gear so we could look for a replacement. Our uncles' mechanic had made a few phone calls with negative results. I finally located a good gear in a junkyard. Uncle Joe approved it, and they reassembled the car and returned it to us.

A few weeks later the rear-end ring gear cracked and locked up the differential. My uncles were able to locate a good used differential assembly and replaced the broken one. In the nine months we had that car, we replaced three rear ends, low gear in the transmission, three or four generators, the water pump, the battery, the starter, and more other parts than I can recall now. We decided to unload the car while everything was working after the third rear-end assembly. In order not to wear out our welcome with our uncles, we did not return to their garage after the first rear-end replacement.

My mechanical experience was limited, and I had few tools, but I purchased a few tools at a time and got some experience. The woman who lived next door had an excellent view of our driveway and, without my realizing it, saw me working on the car many times. She told my parents that she would see me with the wheels off that car and then, a few minutes later, with the car all back together, driving down the street. My brother had no knowledge of or interest in the car except driving it, and I realized that it was up to me to keep the car in good condition.

The city where we lived had a vehicle inspection lane that every car was required to pass twice a year. If the car passed, a decal was put on the windshield, expiring six months from the day it passed. A car that didn't pass was given a temporary sticker expiring in thirty days, during which time the owner was required to get the necessary repairs made and return for reinspection of the unsafe items. When it came time to take the Chevrolet through, I presumed that it would pass. It did not pass, however, because the front brakes did not pull enough pressure on the test machine.

I had already adjusted the brakes to what I considered tight. On the 1929 Chevrolet the front brakes were controlled by rods and levers and could be adjusted without removing the wheels. When I returned to the inspection lane several days later, I tightened the front brakes very tight a few blocks before going back through. This time the inspector passed the car. As soon as I had an opportunity, a few blocks from the inspection lane, I loosened the front brakes the proper amount so that they did not drag. Since we had this car for only nine months it was not necessary to take it through the inspection lane again.

After we had owned this car for only a couple of months I noticed that the driver's seat was suddenly uncomfortable. I undid the backrest upholstery and found that the steel strap, going from each upright piece of the steel frame to the other side, had broken. A trip to a welding shop took care of this, and reassembling the backrest upholstery restored the comfort.

All four tires had the original tread and were good. I had one of the bald 4.50 × 20 tires that came with the car recapped. The art of recapping tires was well known because it had been done extensively on civilian passenger tires during World War II. I had the tire recapped at the Goodrich dealer. I put the freshly recapped tire on the spare. About four months later I noticed that the tread was separating from the casing of the tire. Fortunately, I had kept the receipt for the recap. Because of this and the fact that the tire had never been on the ground, the tire was replaced at no charge and without question.

For the ten years prior to 1929, Chevrolet built cars with four-cylinder engines only, concentrating on low-priced models exclusively since 1922. A few "Classic Six" models and a few V-8 models had been built in the middle teens. Chevrolet's engine with six cylinders proved to be successful. It was modified and improved through the years with Chevrolet still using the same basic six-cylinder engine into the 1960s.

By that time Chevrolet had returned to making some cars with four-cylinder engines and some with V-8 engines.

When Chevrolet brought out its six-cylinder engine for the 1929 model year, it retained the four-cylinder, rear-axle assemblies. They were not strong enough, however, and Chevrolet had considerable trouble with them. It is understandable that two teenaged drivers with only a few years' driving experience could be a little hard on a car, yet it is a poor design that requires them to go through three rear ends in nine months. That was the only car I owned that had any kind of differential or rear-axle problems.

Several years after selling the 1929 Chevrolet the family friend from whom we bought the car told me that he could replace a broken axle shaft (not a complete rear end) in forty-five minutes wherever it broke because he had had so much experience replacing them. He said that he never took the car out unless he had a new spare axle shaft and a wire coat hanger under the front seat in the tool compartment with the rest of the tools. The coat hanger was to hook around the broken axle shaft to fish it out. All the broken axle shafts was one of the big reasons he did not like to drive. As far as I can recall he never had another car.

Like many low-priced cars of the era, this 1929 Chevrolet had an outside gasoline gauge; you had to be outside the car at the gas tank at the rear of the car to read the gauge. If the driver forgot to look at the gauge before he got into the driver's seat he had no way of knowing how much gas he had. The gauge on this particular car was difficult to read because the white gauge face had become stained over the years. The result was that I never knew exactly how much gas was in this car's tank.

For its 1930 models Chevrolet made the change to having the gasoline gauge on the dashboard, the same basic way all cars have had ever since, with an electrical sending unit inside the tank and a read-out unit on the dashboard.

The 1928 model was Chevrolet's first car with brakes on all four wheels instead of on the rear wheels only. The front of the frame, hood, and so on were longer, as if Chevrolet had had plans to introduce its six-cylinder engine in 1928 instead of 1929.

One of the few changes Chevrolet made between its 1929 and 1930 models was to replace the motor-driven "ooga" horn with a vibrator type, which made a "beep" sound. When I seriously considered selling the car I decided to keep the ooga horn because original ones were becoming scarce. I located one of the beep type and switched them. The next owner got a good safe horn, and I kept the ooga. It was one of the few parts of the car that had never given any trouble!

This was my first experience with a car with a four-spoke steering wheel; most cars of that era had that type. It was very strong with a thick rim that a man could grip, but a woman would have trouble getting her fingers all the way around it. Front wheels on a low-priced Chevrolet were far from easy to steer and required both hands to firmly grip the rim to keep the car under control when a front tire would hit a bump or a chuck hole.

As with other cars of this era, the car had only one taillight and one brake light and no turn signals. Since the car had demountable rims, the brake/tail/license plate light were all one fixture, and it was mounted on the bracket inside the spare tire's demountable rim, on the very back of the car. Unfortunately, the lights could be seen only from directly behind the car. A driver in a car in the adjacent lane could not see whether your lights were on. For the 1931 Chevrolet and for every model since, entire wheels, not demountable rims, have been used, and the tail/brake/license plate light has been mounted on the left rear fender. A fancy accessory at that time was to have one for the right rear fender as well. This was an added safety feature.

This car was also my first actual experience with a headlight switch that was activated by flipping up a lever. Eventually I would have a total of six cars with this type of switch. In the early 1930s car designers decided to use a pull-type switch mounted on the dashboard, within easy reach of the driver. This type was retained until the mid 1980s, when the "smart switch" was introduced. The idea was that one would not have to take one's eyes from the road to use the turn signals, turn on the headlights, windshield wipers, cruise control, and so on.

As roads improved and cars could be driven faster in the late 1920s, a subtle change took place in floor boards. Until the mid-1920s cars had three or four floor boards in front; each wooden board was covered with linoleum with aluminum strips as trim around each board. This made the boards easy to remove and reinstall when servicing was necessary under the floor. In the late 1920s the number of front floor boards remained the same, but they were now being covered with a rubber mat with a jute-type backing. In addition to costing the car manufacturer less, the rubber mat kept dirt and drafts from coming up between the boards as well as keeping road and mechanical noises down.

By 1937, when the last U.S. manufacturer converted to all-steel bodies, the floor was also all steel with removable steel inspection plates for checking components located under the floor, such as batteries and master cylinders. After the rubber mat was removed, the steel floor could be unbolted and removed when servicing mechanical parts under the floor was necessary. Technically, the term floor *boards* has been a misnomer since 1937. This 1929 Chevrolet had the "modern" rubber mat covering the front floor boards.

Since the 1910s rear floors have always been covered, either with a rubber mat, on low-priced cars, or carpeting on medium- and high-priced cars. There were no mechanical parts under the rear floor requiring its removal for service.

This car, like many cars of the era, had a windshield that would open slightly. There was a regulator, like a window regulator, inside above the windshield. Turning its crank would make the glass roll up in its tracks about three inches. This allowed all sorts of interesting items and creatures to come inside. Other cars had windshield assemblies hinged at the top, with the bottom able to swing out about three inches. Because of the nature of the system, only enclosed cars could have this feature. In the early 1930s windshields became slanted to achieve streamlining. This meant that by the mid-1930s windshields could no longer be opened. This led to the addition of cowl ventilators and vent glasses in each front-door window. General Motors/Fisher Body called its system "no-draft ventilation."

The windshield and rear glass were parallel in this car and at a ninety-degree angle to the road. At night the headlights from a following car would glare through the inside mirror onto the inside of the windshield, which drivers found very distracting, especially in heavy traffic. I was able to find a plastic accessory in an auto supply store, made of new glareproof material, to eliminate the problem. It clipped over the top of the inside mirror and allowed the driver to see the headlights of following cars without glare. For daytime driving the plastic would flip up and out of the way.

Once while driving this car I knew that I was low on gasoline. I was not near one of the stations where I normally bought gas, but I knew that I could not make it to one of them anyway. I remembered that there was a Studebaker dealer a few blocks away, on my way home.

It had two gasoline pumps out in front, one for regular and one for high-test "ethyl." I drove up to the "regular" pump, and as I reached down to turn off the ignition key the engine stopped running. After buying some gas, at twenty-five cents a gallon, the engine was *very* hard to start, and I had to grind away on the starter for a full minute before the engine caught. What had happened was that I had run out of gas just as I pulled up to the gas pump. The car was hard to start because the fuel pump had to pump some gasoline from the tank up into the carburetor before there was enough gasoline to ignite. That was the only time in my life that I ran out of gas in a gas station!

2 · *1934 Oldsmobile*

Because my brother and I were still under twenty-one when we bought this car, our father put the title and insurance in his name on it, too. He took no interest in this or any of my subsequent cars and never had any occasion to ride in any of them. My brother and I shopped around at some used-car lots and called some private ads. We found this one advertised in the newspaper.

It was a 1934 Oldsmobile four-door touring sedan (which meant that it had a built-in trunk) with the spare tire mounted on the rear, outside the trunk. It had a straight eight-cylinder engine and 7.00 × 16 tires. One of the car's selling points was that it had four new tires and new brakes, including axle seals on all four wheels and the four wheel cylinders rebuilt. Those items gave no problems in the three years (mid-1947 until mid-1950) I had the car.

However, it required two transmission overhauls and an engine overhaul in addition to a couple of generators, alcohol for the radiator, a water pump, a fuel pump, welding of the center steering link bracket back onto the frame a couple of times, and probably other items I have forgotten. I remember that in replacing the double-acting fuel pump I originally connected the hoses wrong. I mistakenly connected the fuel line to the windshield wiper/vacuum side diaphragm, then wondered why the carburetor flooded as soon as the engine started.

For the 1934–1936 models this same straight-eight engine was used in the LaSalle as well as the Oldsmobile. LaSalle returned to a Cadillac-designed V-8 for its 1937 model and used it through 1940, when LaSalle ceased production.

General Motors (GM) began making cars with "knee action" in 1934. That was GM's term for independent front suspension. Each front wheel had its own coil spring and shock absorber and there was no front axle. Chrysler Corporation also had a form of independent front suspension, as did several independent makers. The type used on this Oldsmobile, as well as the Buick and the Cadillac, had center-controlled steering. The steering rod went directly to the center of the car's frame, where it was connected to two tie rods of the same length, one to each front wheel. This made the car very easy to steer. The bracket to the center of the frame would occasionally come loose and have to be welded back together. Modern cars do not use this same design; instead, they have an idler arm that must be replaced periodically when the wear is excessive.

This system worked flawlessly on this car. I never had to have the front wheels aligned, and there was never any pull, and the tire wear was always even.

Oldsmobile and Buick began using hydraulic brakes in 1934. After having this car about eight months I was driving down a long hill into town one day. When I stepped on the brake pedal it went all the way to the floor. I stepped on it a second time, and this time the brakes worked properly. This frightened me considerably, and I had the master cylinder rebuilt right away, even though the brakes worked properly except for that one time. With the master cylinder now rebuilt and the four wheel cylinders being rebuilt just before I got the car, the brake system gave no further problems.

For cars equipped with built-in trunks, 1934 was a transition year. Bolt-on trunks had been available for several years from most auto makers. A built-in trunk, however, was much more streamlined and up to date. Because the spare tire was bolted on the outside of the car's trunk there was a rather small lid directly on top of the trunk; the result was that everything had to be lifted straight up to unload the trunk, which was rather awkward. There were two chrome-plated hinges on the outside. On my many trips to many junkyards I acquired two unbroken hinges for future use. Eventually I used them as, one by one, mine broke. The following model year, 1935, the designers realized that the trunk could easily be made larger to store the spare tire inside. Because the entire back of the trunk could then open up, the trunk became much easier to load and unload.

The framework of the Fisher body was wood with the sheet metal panels tacked on the outside. The one-piece steel "turret top" first appeared in 1935. My 1934 had vent windows in front and vent windows in each quarter panel. It had a cowl ventilator that opened backward so as not to cause a draft on one's feet when it was fully open. In other words, the wide opening was about an inch from the windshield, and the front of the cowl ventilator barely opened.

Standard equipment on that car was a two-piece metal tire cover with the Oldsmobile emblem in the center. That was the only item of original equipment not on the car when I owned it. The spare tire was a spare only, but, since the car came with four brand-new tires, the spare was fortunately never needed as I never had a flat.

The appearance of the 1934 Oldsmobile and all of the General Motors cars was improved over that of the 1933 models although major changes had been made between the 1932 and 1933 models. All GM cars and, for that matter, those of the rest of the U.S. auto industry were given skirts on the rear sections of all four fenders. This was accomplished by adding a triangular piece of metal to the rear portion of each fender. The main part of the front sections was also given a more rounded appearance. The grille work on every 1933 Oldsmobile model was oval and sloped back. The slope appearance was retained for the 1934 models, but the general shape was changed to rectangular.

This car was fairly easy to drive in the snow, probably because it was heavy and had 7.00 × 16 tires, which were considerably wider than the 6.00 × 16 size on most small and medium-size cars of the era. Snow tires were just becoming popular and available, but they were made for 6.00 × 16 size only, which was the same size as for military Jeeps. Jeep tires were strictly for mud and snow, and, although they would fit civilian passenger car wheels, they made an uncomfortable vibration, not noticed in Jeeps. Because the tires on my car were new, the tread was deep, so by doing normal, careful snow driving (namely, "don't do anything suddenly") I was able to get by on those regular tires without chains and without ever getting stuck or bumping into anything.

This car had an unusual headlight arrangement. Beginning in 1932 and going up through the 1939 models, most U.S. auto manufacturers switched from flat headlight lenses to convex lenses for three reasons: (1) Roads and highways were constantly being improved, so they were capable of handling traffic at sixty miles an hour; (2) automobiles had continually been improved so a new (1932) car was capable of operating at sixty miles an hour; and (3) the lighting engineers had recently learned how to diffuse the headlight to illuminate the road and other traffic much better at night without an unnecessary glare to drivers of

The author and his 1934 Oldsmobile.

oncoming cars. It was still necessary to keep the lights in proper aim, however. By the 1934 models, the lenses were about an inch deep.

Another strange item on this model Oldsmobile was the headlight switch. It was on a knob that the driver pulled out, as usual, but the switch had three notches instead of the usual two. The usual two were parking lights on the first notch, then driving lights on the second notch, all the way out. A dimmer switch on the floor allowed the driver to change to high beam when there was no oncoming traffic. This car had three notches: the first for parking, the second notch for city driving, and the third for country driving. I never could see any difference between the "city" and "country" notches, so I usually drove with "country" and still used the dimmer switch. I am not aware of any other cars having this three-position light arrangement for 1934 or any other model.

The following year, 1935, Oldsmobile and all of the GM cars (except the low-priced "standard" Chevrolet) changed bodies considerably. They were given the one-piece steel turret top. All Oldsmobile, Pontiac, and Chevrolet "master" models were also given "suicide" front doors for the 1935 models only. Other U.S. car makers used this type of front door on various models during the mid-1930s.

For its 1934 models Oldsmobile also made a car with a six-cylinder engine, as it did through all the eight-cylinder years. The outward appearance of the 1934 sixes and eights was identical except that on the sixes everything (for example, the body, the fenders, the grilles, the doors, the tires, and, of course, the engine) was slightly smaller. Since the sixes didn't cost as much, they were the higher production of the two. During the time I had this car, the father of a friend of mine dabbled in used cars and made a little extra money. One of the used cars he had for a while was a six-cylinder, 1934 Oldsmobile. Although I never had occasion to ride in it, his car seemed to be about a size smaller overall than mine. Mine had a push button on the left side of the dash for the driver to use to engage the starter; his had a pedal to step on as did most cars of the 1934 era. His car also had two taillights, two windshield wipers and two arm rests, as mine had.

On the front of this car was a "graceful lady" chrome figure on top of the grille panel, showing the lady leaning back. It was bolted to the grille panel at the front end of the center hood hinge, which was also chrome. The 1934 Buick and this Oldsmobile used the same body shell and looked identical from the side with one exception: the lady ornament. On the Buick she leaned forward, whereas on the Oldsmobile she leaned back.

One day I had to have something done on the car that I could not do myself. I took the car to a repair garage near where I worked, where I was assured that the car would be ready late that afternoon and would cost around $15.00. I had used this garage before and had confidence in the repairmen. When I returned later to get the car, I found it parked on the side street in front of the shop, with a dump truck parked in front of my car. As I came closer I saw that my graceful lady was broken off but was still lying on the hood of my car. I picked up the broken piece and went into the shop.

The owner was not there, but the other mechanic said that they had worked on the dump truck that day and that the garage owner had parked the dump truck and apparently hit my graceful lady with the rear-frame cross-member of the truck. I told him that I was prepared to pay the $15.00 repair bill if they would replace my graceful lady. I reminded him that he would have to make several phone calls to locate a good one and then remove the radiator to get access to the mounting bolts, all of which would probably come to more than $15.00. He suggested that I take the car and then stop back in a few days to see how the owner felt about my idea. When I went back later, I was told that if I overlooked the broken graceful lady, they would overlook the $15.00 repair bill. We parted friends, and I used them again on different cars.

After a little over a year of dual ownership of this car with my brother, he told me he needed money for a project in which he was becoming involved. We agreed that he would give me his half of the car for the money. Since the title was still in my father's name, this was just an informal agreement between us. Our parents were aware of the agreement arrangement. I had been keeping the car maintained because my brother, like my father, had no real interest in automobiles. Things worked out very well for my brother, and within a short time he was assigned a company car which he was allowed to use for personal transportation.

In late 1948 I made a compression test on the Oldsmobile and found that the cylinders were uneven. I took it to a mechanic to have the valves ground. At the time (age twenty) I did not have the necessary mechanical experience to tackle such a job myself. After I got the car back it ran beautifully, but I was constantly followed by blue smoke. When I would let up on the accelerator while driving and then press on it again, a giant cloud of blue smoke would come out of the tail pipe. At times I could not see the cars behind me in my mirror.

I knew that I could not continue driving this way as it was a traffic hazard. I presumed that sooner or later a policeman would stop me and give me a ticket. In a few weeks I returned to the mechanic who had ground the valves and had him replace the piston rings, the wrist pins, and the main and connecting rod bearings. I now had a beautiful, sweet-running engine that remained trouble free as long as I had the car, about another eighteen months.

I recall one pleasant summer evening driving home from someone's house on a neighborhood street with a rather high crown in the center. At the intersection of another street, also with a high crown, the car rose from leaning to the right, to level, then back to leaning to the right, when everything died. The engine died, the lights went out and all I could do was to coast to the side of the road. Thankfully, I was not blocking traffic or anyone's driveway. The next morning I called AAA (my parents were still members) and had the car towed to the nearest repair shop, which just happened to be an Oldsmobile dealer. When I went to get the car the next day, I learned that the fifteen-year-old positive battery cable insulation had rubbed through from where it went through the frame, from the battery box under the front seat to the starter. When the cable touched the frame, the battery shorted and the lights went out. Naturally, I was charged "drug store" price for the new cable and battery.

During the winter of 1947–1948 I was coming home about 7:00 P.M. one night. It was already dark. This cooling system would not hold permanent antifreeze so I had alcohol in the radiator. On this night I was about half a mile from home when I suddenly smelled hot alcohol. I stopped and raised the left side of the hood but, with the aid of only a nearby street light, saw nothing wrong. I went on home, and as I gunned the engine to start up the steep part of the driveway the engine stopped. Fire appeared under the hood! I ran into the house and called the fire department.

It turned out that the top radiator hose had split and leaked enough alcohol on top of the hot exhaust manifold and cylinder head to burn. As I started up the steep driveway and gunned the engine, the surging water pump sprayed hot alcohol onto the hot engine parts. By the time the fire department arrived the alcohol had already stopped burning. All they had to do was to douse everything and disconnect the battery.

Since this car was carried on the insurance policy as a second car, it had the same coverage as the family car, including fire insurance. When the car was ready a couple of weeks later, the top sections of the hood had been refinished and the car ran very well.

Everything on top of the flathead straight-eight engine burned, including the carburetor, the distributor, and the associated wiring; even the paint on the hood was blistered from heat. My father was employed in a managerial capacity at the company where he worked. It had about a dozen vehicles, and one of my father's responsibilities was deciding where to insure the vehicles. My father also had his own car insured with the same insurance company for several years before my brother and I were old enough to drive.

In the three or four years between the time my brother and I first had a car until we turned twenty-one, the two cars we had were carried on the family car policy as a second car with two teenaged drivers who had learned to drive at the local AAA club. I do not know this for a fact, but it would not surprise me if the adjuster was told to treat this car "right" as it belonged to the children of a man who had direct responsibility to decide where a dozen or so vehicles would be insured. Perhaps that is why any item that might have been questionable on someone else's car was taken care of on this car without question and with no depreciation.

By the summer of 1950 I had acquired a couple of early 1920s cars and decided to sell this 1934 Oldsmobile while everything was still working properly. I sold it to a friend of a friend. The last I heard of the car was that it had met an unglamorous end when the fellow who bought it had a few too many beers one Saturday night and decided to see how fast it would go. He found out the hard way when one of the connecting rods came through the side of the block!

3 · *1925 Dodge Brothers*

In the summer of 1949 I saw a 1925 Dodge Brothers roadster advertised in the Sunday newspaper. I went to see it and couldn't get over how cute it was. It was the Special series, meaning that it had the accessories of five disc wheels (instead of wooden wheels with demountable rims); front and rear full bumpers instead of no bumpers at all; nickel-plated radiator shell instead of painted black; cowl lights instead of none; and a transmission lock instead of none. All this, but no shock absorbers. The odometer showed 32,000 miles, which the present owner presumed to be correct. The fenders were somewhat dented; the original gas tank cap was missing and a substitute was in its place; the original paint was fair with a little of the original stripe still showing; the paint on the fenders and wheels was poor. The top looked to be original, or at least had been in place for many years. I am sure that the side curtains were original.

There was a very minor crack in the water jacket on the outside of the engine cylinder block at the left rear corner. To repair it would have involved removing the engine, then welding it properly. The crack was only on the outside, so there was no imminent danger as the running of the car was not affected. The present owner had added "stop leak," and the crack was not leaking at the time. It gave no trouble as long as I owned the car. I was fascinated by the backward gearshift; the combination starter-generator; the twelve-volt electrical system; the distributor driven off the water pump, both mounted on the side of the engine; the absence of an intake manifold with the updraft carburetor bolted directly to the side of the engine block; and the float-type oil gauge with no dip stick. These were all new to me.

The author's 1925 Dodge Brothers roadster before the new top and correct-size tires were installed.

Dodge Brothers Shift Pattern

Dodge Brothers used this shift pattern on all its cars until its 1927 models. The Buick and Reo patterns were the exact opposite of this Dodge Brothers pattern: Where Dodge Brothers had first gear (low), Buick and Reo had second; where Dodge Brothers had high; Buick and Reo had second, and so on. Franklin also used the Buick/Reo shift pattern for several years.

All roadsters and touring cars of this era had no locks on the doors; they would have been useless because the car bodies were completely open. This roadster had a lock on the trunk as standard equipment. Touring cars did not have trunks, so valuables could not be locked up. This car also had an accessory transmission lock. The only thing it would do was to lock the transmission in neutral. A professional thief could easily hotwire the ignition to start the engine, but with the transmission locked in neutral he could not drive the car away. The lock was on the transmission next to the shift lever (stick). It was even with the floor, so it was subject to getting dirty. The correct key came with my car, and it worked but was very stiff and hard to turn. I did not use it because it might have stuck in the locked position where I could not drive the car. The trunk lock worked properly all the time.

About four blocks from where I lived was a mechanic who had a small one-man shop with a pit behind his home. His father had been there before as a mechanic, so he was "grandfathered in" as far as all the zoning laws were concerned. Around 1930 he purchased a used 1925 Dodge Brothers standard coupe from the local gas company when the company decided to replace it. My friend, or his father, put a big wide board across the original front bumper to push disabled cars. He also opened the trunk lid and bolted what appeared to be a homemade, hand-operated crane on the back of the coupe to tow a car.

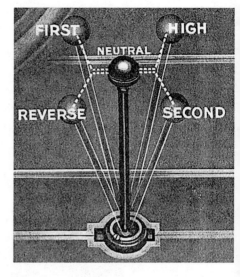

Dodge Brothers Motor Vehicles gear shift lever positions.

When I met him he was using the coupe strictly as an errand car. He had been drafted into the army during World War II when he was almost too old for the draft. He was made an aircraft mechanic and spent the war years rebuilding airplane engines. After his discharge he bought an army surplus Dodge Command car. For civilian use these vehicles were like a modern-day power wagon. It looked like a modern-day Jeep station wagon but without any comforts. It had two full bench seats and carrying load space behind the rear seat. He used this as a service car. With its four-wheel drive it did the job for him. Without this man I don't know how I would have kept this or my subsequent Dodge Brothers cars running.

Through the years he had scrapped a few old Dodge Brothers cars and kept the parts he expected to need in the future. He brought out just what I needed on many occasions.

It was the nature of this Dodge Brothers roadster of mine for the brakes to squeal badly when applied hard. They were quiet in normal operation, however. On more than one occasion I would see another car wanting to cross in front of me, whether from a stop sign or a driveway. The driver would look my way and see my old Dodge Brothers and think, "I can beat that old rattletrap," and pull out in front of me. I would then jam on the brakes as hard as I could to make them squeal. Then the other driver would presume I couldn't stop and zoom out of the way.

JOHNSON TRANSMISSION
LOCK saves 15% on theft
insurance. Approved by
Underwriters' Laborator-
ies, Inc., and recommend-
ed by us to every DODGE
BROTHERS car owner.

Price **$15.00**

"It Locks the Gears"

JOHNSON
LOCKS
are
installed
by our
SERVICE
STATION

In the spring of 1950 there was a bad windstorm while this car was sitting outside. The top was ripped in several places, especially where it had been tacked to the body behind the seat. The insurance policy I had covered windstorm damage so I called the company. It sent an adjuster, who allowed me $75.00 on the cost of the $110.00 top. Had I had the extra money at the time, I would have had the side curtains replaced at the same time, to make a much nicer-looking job.

All Dodge Brothers cars from the 1915 model through the 1926 model had a combination starter-generator. It cranked the engine, as a starter, from the front of the engine's crankshaft to the starter-generator unit. Since the chain ran in the engine's oil, the unit did not make any noise. You had to be within about a foot of the engine to hear the unit operate.

At the time I bought this car the fellow who lived next door worked the graveyard shift from 11:00 PM to 7:00 AM and usually arrived home about fifteen minutes before I left for my job. About ten days or so after I began using this car he sought me out one Saturday. He asked me about the car because he said that he would be getting into bed every morning about fifteen minutes before I would leave for work. He said he would hear me close my door, then hear the engine running and me drive away. He asked me why he never heard the starter. I opened the hood and showed him everything and had him listen closely while I stepped on the starter button with the ignition off so he could hear how the starter system operated. Then I turned on the ignition so he could hear how fast the engine started. I presume he relaxed and slept better after that since that mystery was now solved for him.

When I bought this car I did not realize that the left running board had deteriorated. It had a dark linoleum mat that hid the condition until one day I stepped down on it and my foot kept going on down. For the next few days I stepped over it. The first chance I had I removed it and measured everything. Replacing it merely required getting a new board cut to size, drilling holes in the proper places for new carriage bolts and reinstalling everything on the brackets riveted to the car's frame to support the running board. For some reason I could not locate a mat or cover for it, so I painted the new running board black. Eventually I found a piece of mat and glued it in place.

Like all Dodge Brothers roadsters and touring cars and several other makes of cars of the era, this car had brackets to hold the top when it was folded down. There was a handle to open on each side of the car; the top was then lowered, and the metal top framework rested in the brackets, and then each bracket was closed. This held the top steady so the material would not chafe against anything. Holding the top steady also prevented the top from stretching under its own weight. A few years later these brackets became unnecessary as bodies became wider. On these 1920s and earlier cars, the top was wider than the body and stacked outside the body. As bodies have been getting wider through the years, convertible tops of the twenty-first century actually stack inside the width of the convertible's body.

A high school near where I worked offered evening auto mechanic classes for about two hours a night, three times a week. I took the class for two semesters. Basically it involved tearing down and rebuilding engines that had been donated by local dealers or repair shops. Since no donations of rear axles, brakes, steering, or transmissions had been made, no courses were available to learn about them "hands on." The teacher would show how to fix one of these components when a student brought one in for repair, presumably from his own car or the family car.

During one of these classes I had to replace the cylinder head gasket on my car. Since the head bolts and spark plugs are out in the open and easily accessible, I was able to do the job in one class session. The teacher also showed me how to clean the carbon from the tops of the pistons and valves and the bottom of the cylinder head. The other class members were also fascinated by the cute things about this car. While replacing the cylinder head gasket I found that the Dodge Brothers had made the engine so that the pistons came all the way to the top of the cylinders. Because the top piston rings came even with the top of the block, a ridge was prevented from forming inside the cylinder. On other cars a ridge would form as the cylinders wore in normal use. A special tool, called a ridge reamer, had to be used on other cars to remove this ridge before the pistons would come out for overhaul.

Once, while visiting a junkyard, I saw a set of five high-tread 6.00 × 20 matched tires on an old Buick. They were much better than the 4.50 × 20 undersized tires on the car at the time. After I replaced them, the front end developed a shimmy. I took the car to my friend to see if he had old balancing equipment or suggestions. He said that the factory fix, back when those cars were new, was to tip the front axle slightly by inserting shims between the axle and the front springs to put the king pins at a slight angle of two degrees. He had a set of the shims, and they worked. He also showed me how to adjust the front axle king pins when they started to wear and become loose.

Eventually the vacuum tank on this car developed a leak in the vacuum system and would not pull the gasoline up from the gas tank at the rear of the car. This causes the engine to run out of gas. Since parts were no longer available to repair these vacuum tanks, I went to my friendly mechanic a few blocks away. He had one that worked and replaced my bad one. When that one eventually went bad, the only solution was to install a twelve-volt electric fuel pump. It is possible to drive a car a few blocks at a time even with a bad vacuum tank. One takes the top off the bad tank and pours about a pint of gasoline into it. This will run the engine for a few blocks. Obviously this cannot be done in heavy traffic or on busy streets.

Vacuum Fuel System

Until the invention of the mechanical fuel pump in the mid-1920s, most cars used this basic method of moving the fuel from the tank at the rear of the car to the carburetor on the engine. The unused engine vacuum went to the tank mounted on the engine and through a float and levers. Gasoline was drawn into the tank and then flowed by gravity down to the carburetor on the side of the engine. The system worked reasonably well for the slow-speed engines of the times. The following drawing shows the Dodge Brothers system.

Replacing the tires turned out to be quite a job. Like some trucks, the tires on disc wheels have a steel retaining ring to hold the outer edge of the tire to the outer edge of the wheel. The inner edge of the wheel has a wider diameter to hold on the inner edge of the tire. This locking/retaining ring is a wedge between the tire and the wheel. There is a notch in the end of the retaining ring to allow for the tire tool to be pushed in and to pry out the edge of the locking/retaining ring from the wheel.

The tire must already have all the air removed and the wheel off the car and lying on the floor, outside up. The end of the ring is pried up, and a tire tool is inserted between the locking/retaining ring and the wheel. A second tire tool is placed a few inches further on, and this process is continued all the way around the wheel until the locking/retaining ring comes completely off.

The old tire and inner tube and flap are now easily removed so that the wheel can be cleaned and the flap and new tire and inner tube can be replaced. The locking/retaining ring is then wedged between the tire and the wheel the opposite way it was removed. When it finally clicks into place, the tire is on properly and ready to inflate, and the wheel can be installed back on the car. To do this on all five wheels, one right after the other, is quite a sweat producer but also brings on a nice sense of accomplishment.

As with many roadsters and touring cars of the 1920s, the windshield was on a slant, tilted in a few degrees from the top. This gave a little streamlining because passing air currents were pushed up slightly while driving. Most of these cars also had a two-piece windshield, upper and lower. The upper piece came about two thirds of the way down from the top; the lower piece came up from the cowl about one third of the way. They did not touch, and a piece of weatherstrip between them theoretically kept rainwater from passing between the two panes of glass.

On all open cars, roadsters, and touring cars, the upper section was pivoted about one third of the way down from the top so that it would swing in or out to provide ventilation as desired. Many open cars of the era also had an arrangement in which the bottom third of the windshield could also be pivoted in or out.

This 1925 Dodge Brothers roadster had both arrangements. Pulling the lower windshield to pivot in directed air down on one's knees and lower legs, which provided a delightful breeze in warm weather. There was a piece of T-shaped weatherstrip rubber between the bottom section and the cowl which was supposed to keep out rainwater. The side curtains were anchored to the windshield post and extended a little further in to cover the gap between the windshield posts and the windshield panes themselves.

There was also an automatic windshield cleaner on the car. It was a vacuum-operated windshield wiper for the driver's side only. The vacuum was drawn directly from the engine, like the gasoline vacuum tank, and a small metal line ran from the engine through the firewall and then through the cowl at the left windshield post, then up the post to the wiper motor, mounted on top of the upper windshield section.

The motor had an off/on switch. The vacuum for the wiper motor had to compete with the vacuum needed to operate the vacuum tank for the gasoline. The gasoline vacuum tank pipe from the engine was

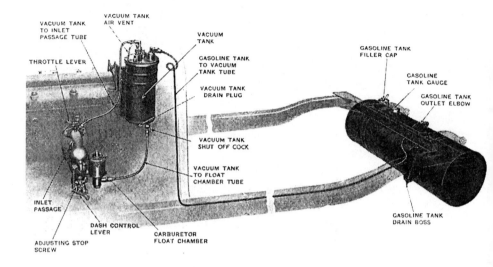

VACUUM TANK
TO INLET
PASSAGE TUBE

VACUUM TANK
AIR VENT

VACUUM
TANK

THROTTLE LEVER

GASOLINE TANK
TO VACUUM
TANK TUBE

VACUUM TANK
DRAIN PLUG

GASOLINE TANK
FILLER CAP

GASOLINE
TANK GAUGE

GASOLINE TANK
OUTLET ELBOW

VACUUM TANK
SHUT OFF COCK

VACUUM TANK
TO FLOAT
CHAMBER TUBE

INLET
PASSAGE

GASOLINE TANK
DRAIN BOSS

DASH CONTROL
LEVER

ADJUSTING STOP
SCREW

CARBURETOR
FLOAT CHAMBER

Gasoline System

much shorter and wider, so the gasoline supply was always adequate. After the vacuum tank went bad and was replaced with the electric fuel pump, the only vacuum line went from the engine directly to the wiper motor. Like all vacuum-operated windshield wipers, the wiper hesitated when you stepped down hard on the gas pedal. When you let up again, the engine could pull down more vacuum, and the wiper would move again.

I drove this car as daily transportation for about a year. Since side curtains have no insulating value at all, winter driving was not too pleasant. This car did not have a heater, so I located a normal hot-water heater and installed it. To get as much heat as possible I made the hoses as part of the engine's cooling system. This required removing a section of the upper radiator hose, then installing two reducer adapters to go from the radiator hose size down to the heater hose size and back again (one going into the heater and one coming out). It was a poor arrangement at best, mainly because the side curtains were very drafty because they did not fit well. Most side curtains did not fit well on cars of this era. In the spring I took all the hoses off and replaced the top radiator hose with one of the proper size.

I met another fellow who had a small electrical supply business. When I learned that he had genuine original NorthEast brand ignition points, condenser, coil, rotor, distributor cap, and so on for my car, I bought them at once. I also put several other people who were restoring other old cars in touch with him.

The city where I grew up had a vehicle inspection station, and every car was required to pass inspection every six months. I was confident that my 1925 Dodge Brothers would pass or I would not have taken it through. The car owner walks alongside the car while a city employee drives the car through the test stations. I had to show the city employee where to put the gearshift lever to get low gear (not reverse). When he raised the front end to check the steering and suspension, I showed him that there were no front brakes. He was impressed when the brake machine did not register any pressure for front wheels and registered almost as much for only the rear wheels as a modern (1950) car with regular hydraulic brakes with drums on all four wheels would register.

The last item he checked was the headlight aim. One of mine was slightly off. The inspector walked from the headlight machine up to my car, looked around and did not see his supervisor, so he grabbed the headlight in question and gave it a good healthy twist. Then he walked back to the machine and pronounced that the car passed.

During the two years I owned his car I also bought cars #4, #5, #6, and #7 and had a disappointing surprise. The surprise was that I was drafted for the Korean War despite an eye problem. One eye went bad in a matter of months while the other remained normal. I had to arrange storage for three 1920s model cars for an unknown length of time. My brother helped considerably while I was away. It wasn't until all my training was completed and I was preparing for shipment overseas that the Army realized that I had been telling the truth all along about my bad eye. Had I realized I would be drafted I would never had bought cars #4, #6, and #7. I sold the 1925 Dodge Brothers in late 1951 after receiving my honorable discharge. I heard later that it was eventually sold to someone in the Florida panhandle.

4 • *1921 Ford*

Shortly after buying the 1925 Dodge Brothers roadster (#3), I found a 1921 Ford roadster in a vacant lot behind a grocery store. There was no top, and there was a big hole in the left side of the engine block. The rest of the car seemed complete although the paint was bad. The tires and upholstery were fair, but usable. A few days earlier I had seen a 1925 Ford Tudor (Ford's way of saying "two-door sedan") in a farmer's field. The grocery store owner told me that he had used the Ford to deliver groceries until it threw the rod through the side of the block; the car cost me $20.00, and a friend and I pushed it to a rented garage. The farmer's engine cost me $10.00, and I borrowed a friend's truck to haul it to the garage. The farmer's engine had the starter, generator, and transmission still attached, just the way it came out of the car. I removed the bad engine and junked it, keeping what few good parts it had.

This was the first car I owned where I took the (1921) engine out of the car and took the (1925) engine apart myself. I had a lot of help overhauling it and getting it back together right. While I was doing this I learned how poorly designed the Model T Ford was, especially the brakes and steering. Technically, the Model T Ford had an emergency brake, but it, too, was ineffective and might hold a Ford if it was already stopped and on a level place with no wind. After the overhaul was completed I put the 1925 engine in the 1921 roadster.

All the work I did on this Model T came in quite handy about twenty-five years later when the man I worked for bought a 1915 Model T Ford touring car to play with. It would not stay running, and his mechanic did not know how to work on this car. My boss had a seventeen-year-old son whom he took along every time he wanted to drive

35

the car. When it would stop running, the son would be assigned crank- ing duties. The 1915 Model T Fords did not come factory equipped with starters; they all had to be cranked. After about ten minutes enough gasoline would flow past the kink in the gasoline pipe so that the engine would start and run for a few more minutes. I volunteered to look at my employer's car. I set all the adjustments (including all those on the four vibrator coils, etc.) to where they belonged. Then I found that the gasoline pipe from the bottom of the tank to the carburetor was kinked where it turned to connect to the carburetor. I replaced the pipe and the car then ran beautifully.

I kept my 1921 roadster for only about a year because it needed the same appearance restoration as the 1925 Dodge Brothers roadster (#3), and I liked the latter a lot better.

This 1921 Ford roadster ran well for a Model T, and after I learned all of its idiosyncrasies I enjoyed driving it around because it was so different. At the time, I also had #2, the 1934 Oldsmobile, and #3, the 1925 Dodge Brothers. Each car had a different type of gearshift.

Model T Ford Transmission

Ford used this transmission in all its Model T cars and trucks from its 1909 models until the end of Model T production in early 1927. The following phantom drawing shows a ring gear on the flywheel to accom- modate a starter, first in production on a Ford in 1919. This was oper- ated by three pedals, not by a lever in the middle of the floor. The left pedal engaged the slow-speed drum, the center pedal engaged the reverse drum, and the right pedal engaged the brake drum. Each pedal, when depressed by the driver, operated a band which squeezed against a particular drum. Ford switched to the shift pattern established by the Society of Automotive Engineers beginning with its Model A models.

The part marked "brake drum" was the brake for the rear wheels. It is inside the transmission, so every part of the Ford between this brake drum and the rear wheels was also a part of the braking system. The bands are not shown in this drawing. When the driver pressed the appropriate pedal, the band to which it was connected squeezed (con- tracted) its drum to apply either low gear, reverse, or the brake.

The Model T Ford was a unique car for its time. It was introduced as a 1909 model in October 1908. By that time the planetary-type trans-

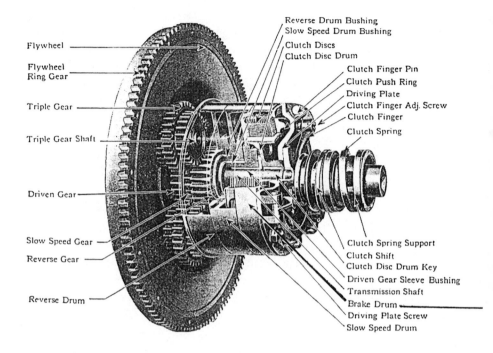

Flywheel

Flywheel
Ring Gear

Triple Gear

Triple Gear Shaft

Driven Gear

Slow Speed Gear

Reverse Gear

Reverse Drum

Reverse Drum Bushing
Slow Speed Drum Bushing
Clutch Discs
Clutch Disc Drum
Clutch Finger Pin
Clutch Push Ring
Driving Plate
Clutch Finger Adj. Screw
Clutch Finger
Clutch Spring

Clutch Spring Support
Clutch Shift
Clutch Disc Drum Key
Driven Gear Sleeve Bushing
Transmission Shaft
Brake Drum
Driving Plate Screw
Slow Speed Drum

Cutaway view of Model T Ford transmission showing one brake drum to stop both rear wheels.

mission had given way to the much more dependable sliding gear-type transmission, where the gears meshed directly and the driver moved a lever to slide the gears out of mesh with one and into mesh with another. Only one other manufacturer introduced a car with a planetary transmission in the United States as late as 1908, and it ceased production in 1910. Planetary was the only type of transmission Ford knew how to build. The previous Ford models (the A, the B, the C, the E, the F, the K, the N, the R, and the S) all had planetary transmission dating back to the founding of the Ford Motor Company in mid-1903. Even then, Ford did not get it right.

When Henry Ford built his first car in 1896 he called it a quadricycle, and it had no reverse gear. If you wanted to back up, you had to push the car backward. It wasn't that Henry Ford forgot to make a reverse gear, he simply didn't know how. When he designed the first car for the Ford Motor Company in 1903, he used a reverse mechanism designed by someone else. When the someone else, Frederick W. Ball, found out about it, he took Henry Ford to court for patent infringement.

Part of the settlement required For to pay Ball $1.00 for each automobile Ford built with Ball's reversing mechanism. The Model T continued to use a planetary transmission. As the Model T became more successful, Ford was irked to have to continue to pay Ball. Eventually Ford had his lawyer negotiate a lump sum settlement with Ball after having paid him hundreds of thousands of dollars over the years.

Ford's idea was to make automobiles as cheaply as possible to keep the price down so more people could afford to buy one. A metallurgist who worked for him, C. Harold Wills, unlocked the secret of making vanadium steel. This made iron and steel parts *very* strong. The process had been known, but the Europeans who developed it kept their secret very closely guarded and priced anything made of vanadium steel out of reach. Wills's discovery made it possible to use vanadium steel in a low-priced car, such as a Ford. Axles and many engine and chassis parts were made with this material. Unfortunately, the best steel in the world did not compensate for the poor and outdated design of the Model T.

Ford could have designed the Model T with one brake at each rear wheel, as other U.S. auto makers had been doing. Instead, Ford had its one and only brake inside the planetary transmission. This meant that the transmission and every part of the chassis between the transmission and the rear tires (such as the universal joint, drive shaft, differential gears and bearings, axles, rear wheel bearings) were all part of the brake system. If one of these parts should fail (not all were made of vanadium steel) or become worn, it would not be able to stop the vehicle. In addition, the brake band inside the planetary transmission was too small. It was smaller than one brake on a regular car of the era having brakes on each rear wheel. This meant that the Ford brake wore out considerably faster than that of another make of car of the same size. Further, with only one brake inside the transmission, the Ford was more likely to skid on a wet street. The action of the differential applies power, whether driving power or braking power, through the wheel where there is the least resistance. On a wet slippery street, one rear wheel could go backward while the other continued to go frontward, causing the Ford to skid sideways. Cars with one brake on *each* rear wheel had braking power applied to each rear wheel only, not to the differential.

As police departments were becoming motorized, the Model T Ford roadster appealed to many cities because of its low price. If a suspect had to be brought to the police station for questioning, the officer would call for a "paddy wagon" or other transportation. Because the Model T was so poorly designed and cheaply built, maintenance and repairs were needed often. Police departments eventually realized that the amount of money they were spending on repairs and "down time" soon cost them more than the price of the car.

Henry Ford had a basic rule concerning improvements to the Model T: If it cost more or took more time, he was not interested. He would allow improvements or changes *only* when forced to by competition. One example is the brass radiator, which was last used on the 1916 model. It was out of date and also too small for the amount of heat the engine had to dissipate. The new steel radiator was painted black instead of being brass. At the same time the brass hub caps were changed from nickel-plated to steel, and the brass rims around the headlights were also changed to steel. The amount of brass on various parts of the car had been cut every year since 1910 to keep the cost down.

Another of Ford's holdouts was the starter. Every other U.S. automobile was equipped with a starter or offered one as an extra-cost option, except Ford — until 1919. The company finally realized that women, who were about to be granted the right to vote, would not buy a car without a starter, so a starter was offered as an accessory beginning in 1919. On every make of car, the starter is just one of several necessary components. A battery is needed to furnish electricity to operate the starter, and a generator is needed to keep the battery charged. A switch is also needed to cause the starter to engage to make the engine's internal parts revolve. Some manufacturers used a combination starter-generator using only one large electric motor. The two-unit system of a separate generator and starter motor was the better system. Since the starter needs a battery, electric lights and a horn can also be used on the car.

No one likes to change a flat tire, and many women at that time did not know how to go about it. Because driving on a flat tire is dangerous (the car is hard to steer and to stop, and driving with a flat destroys both the tire and tube), the tire and inner tube had to be patched on the spot where the tire went flat. Carrying a spare tire and tube on an extra rim meant that the flat tire, inner tube and rim could be removed as a unit and a good, already inflated spare unit could be installed in its place. Ford used different sizes of tires on the front and the rear; they were not interchangeable. The front tire size was 30 × 3 (24-inch diameter), and the rear size was 30 × 3½ (23-inch diameter).

Photograph showing ball and socket steering linkage with no gears or gear box.

Fronts were three inches wide, making them slightly easier to steer than the three-and-one-half-inch rears. With the demountable rims all were standardized at 30 × 3½. Eventually Ford offered demountable rims as an accessory with all tires the same size so that only one spare had to be carried and would fit either front or rear. For reasons never explained, starter equipment and demountable rims were sold by Ford as a package only.

My 1921 roadster had the starter and demountable rim accessory package. By 1921 the popularity of a starter and demountable rims had grown, and many, many retail customers bought them even though they raised the price of the Ford. Because many World War I veterans came home in 1919 and 1920 and sought civilian jobs, 1921 was a depression year. Also, the war industry jobs ended, and people who had held them were mostly laid off at the end of the war. Like other U.S. car makers Ford reduced production and cut prices until business picked up again. Oddly enough, 1923 was Ford's best year, selling over three million Model T's. Then the bottom fell out of the Model T market as sales steadily declined.

The steering, which was just as unsafe as the brake system, had

View from under right side of a Model T Ford showing upper and lower spigots near bottom rear of flywheel cover of crank case. Spigots must be opened to see if oil runs out; this is the way the engine oil was checked.

only a ball-and-socket connection between the bottom of the steering column and the tie rod arm. Since it was only a few inches from the ground it was subject to dirt and mud, especially in the ball-and-socket joint, causing wear. Trying to keep the parts lubricated was futile because they accumulated so much dirt and mud. Ford's suggestion was to disassemble the ball-and-socket joint and file down the socket to again achieve a tight connection. If the socket was filed down a tiny bit too much it would bind, locking the steering. The result was that there was a lot of bending and lost motion in the steering rods because of the ball-and-socket system. Every other U.S. auto manufacturer used a steering gear box securely bolted to the car frame at the bottom of the steering column. This gave a positive, firm connection, eliminating the binding and lost motion of the Model T Ford system.

One of the first things one must do in removing the engine from a car is to remove the radiator. While I had the radiator out of the 1921 I had a radiator shop clean it and repair any leaks. On the Model T Ford the engine and transmission come out as one unit. It is much easier to reline the transmission bands while the transmission is already out of the car, so that is what I did.

The Model T had a unique way of checking the oil: There was no dip stick! The engine crank case, to which the engine and transmission were bolted, contained two spigots, one about two inches directly above the other. The ideal amount of oil was halfway between the two spigots. In order to turn each spigot one had to get under the car with pliers or something similar, and turn the spigots enough to see when oil flowed out. If no oil flowed out of the lower spigot you added about a quart of oil. If oil flowed out the top spigot you let it flow until it stopped flowing.

Rather than get under the car every time you needed to check the oil, many people would take an old broom handle and cut a lengthwise slot in the end of it to fit the spigot handle, then get down on one knee and turn the spigots from the right center edge of the car, using the old broom handle to reach them. Many gas station attendants used a piece of pipe with a slot cut in the end instead of an old broom handle to check the oil for Ford customers.

One had to remember to be sure both spigots were closed prior to starting the engine, otherwise all the oil would be thrown out by the internal engine parts revolving in just a few minutes.

Since my 1921 roadster was factory equipped with the starter arrangement, it did not have a problem with headlights. Cars that were not so equipped used the engine's magneto to supply the electric current to the headlights. The faster the engine ran, the brighter were the headlights. The magneto lights required special bulbs. The starter-equipped cars came with an electric taillight; the magneto-only cars came equipped with an oil taillight which worked on the same principle as a lantern. The oil taillight had to be filled with oil and lighted with a match.

This was the only car I ever owned that did not have a bumper, either front or rear. Bumpers were considered accessories on almost all cars until about 1930. The original owner of this Model T did not buy either bumper. Ford did not make an accessory bumper in 1921, so the owner would have had to go to an auto accessory store to buy them, then install them himself or have a mechanic do so. The original owner of my 1923 Dodge Brothers bought a front bumper only; the shape of the rear springs acted as sort of a rear bumper. The owner of my 1923 Lincoln, 1925 Dodge Brothers and 1929 Chevrolet all bought both front and rear bumper assemblies when the cars were new.

This Model T, like every other one, did not have a gasoline gauge.

The gas tank was under the driver's seat; its cushion had to be removed every time the driver bought gasoline. The tank was round and held ten gallons. The tank was mounted on top of the car's frame, and the gasoline flowed by gravity to the carburetor on the right side of the engine. There was no way of telling how much gasoline was in the tank. What most owners did was to get a flat stick, like a paint stirrer but about fifteen inches long and about an inch wide, and dip it in the tank to see how wet it was with gasoline when they pulled it out. The flat stick could be kept under the seat alongside the tank opening where it could be handy yet out of the way. Many Ford dealers and oil companies, gas stations, and so on gave these out gratis to Ford owners.

The very last Model Ts had the gas tank mounted on the cowl. There was a door on top of the cowl that looked like a cowl ventilator. Under that door was the cap for the gasoline tank.

5 • *1923 Dodge Brothers*

In late 1949, after having sold #4, I saw a 1923 Dodge Brothers touring car in the parking lot of an auto repair shop. I knew the people there and asked them about the car. I was told that they had been keeping the car running for several years for the original owner, an elderly furniture upholsterer. Now, however, the ring gear in the differential (rear end) had broken, and they did not know where to find a good one for a replacement. The owner would have liked to have the car fixed because it was the only car he knew how to drive.

The appearance of the car was something right out of *Tobacco Road*. The only accessory the car had was a dented front bumper. All five tires were the "maypop" variety. They may pop at any minute. They were four ply, and three of the four plies were showing through on every tire; I have never seen tires so badly worn yet still holding air. Several years earlier the owner had someone cut the back body panel with a cutting torch and put two hinges at the bottom and a chain at each upper corner. He used this as a tailgate to carry long pieces of furniture to his shop to reupholster. He also cut the top material directly above the tailgate so it would be out of the way and flap in the breeze. Apparently no one had taken any interest in this car for quite some time. The owner probably was unable to wash it, and his adult children had other things to do. I am convinced that all that was done for this car was to buy gasoline for it. The engine started right up but was very noisy. I was afraid to race it for fear something might come apart inside.

The 1923 Dodge Brothers was somewhat of a transition model. It had outside door handles, so you did not have to reach inside, over the top of the door, to use the catch to open the door. Also, the radiator

Top: The author's 1923 Dodge Brothers touring car, from the original owner.
   Bottom: The author's 1923 Dodge Brothers touring car; the spare tire was originally mounted on the rear of the car.

was slightly taller, giving it more capacity; the hood had to be a little taller as well. The rear springs were the old-fashioned, scroll-type, three-quarter elliptic. This was the last year Dodge Brothers, or anyone else, would use that type of spring because it was now out of style. That type of spring had been used on fancy horse-drawn carriages to give a smoother ride and carried over to automobiles but was no longer needed to give a smooth ride. The following year, for the 1924 models, the frame and the rest of the chassis were lowered, and semi-elliptic rear springs were adopted, the same type as the rest of the U.S. auto industry was already using.

The wheels were also made smaller. They went from the high-pressure, 25-inch diameter, 33 × 4 size to the balloon 20-inch, 32 × 6 (6.00 × 20) size to produce an easier ride. The same basic engine, transmission, and rear axle styles were retained.

From previous experience I knew of a junkyard about 25 miles out in the country that still had a few old Dodge Brothers vehicles, and I was confident that I could find a good rear axle/differential there. The car owner's children wanted him to give up that old touring car because repair parts were no longer available. I also think that they didn't want him driving a car that looked so disreputable. They bought him a 1939 Plymouth coupe with the gearshift on the steering column and were trying to teach him the gearshift pattern, which was considerably different from the old Dodge Brothers shift pattern on the floor.

I had not told anyone about the junkyard in the country. Meanwhile I bought the car for $30.00 and had it towed to a garage I had rented. I then bought the used rear end assembly and had a mechanic help me replace it and reline the (rear) brakes while the rear end was out. We also overhauled the engine, and I had the radiator cleaned out and any leaks repaired. The mechanic could work on my car only when he had no customers' cars to fix, so overhauling the engine and replacing the rear end took about three weeks. The engine noises were corrected by having the pistons knurled and filing down the shims on the main and connecting rod bearings until the clearance between the bearings and the crankshaft was correct. When this mechanical work was finished the car ran beautifully and quietly.

Then I had a body man weld the rear body panel back in place where it had been torched apart many years earlier. He leaded things in as best he could, but lumps and waves were still visible. Fiberglass resin repair materials were not available in 1949–1950. The pictures were taken after the rear panel had been welded back in place.

The tires on this car were so bad that I was half afraid to drive it. I knew that replacing them had to be the next thing I would have to do to it. My only problem was that I already owned three 1920s cars, all of which needed attention. This car had to go into storage for the time I was away in the Army. When I returned I realized that I owned too many old cars and very reluctantly sold it to a Dodge dealer about 75 miles away. Part of the deal was that I was to deliver it there. There was an old car show the following weekend about 75 miles further. Friends agreed to go slightly out of their way and pick me up at the Dodge dealer so that I could ride to the show and back with them. I left very early in the morning to allow time for changing a flat tire or something. I told the friends the exact route I would be taking, and they agreed to take the same route and watch for me in case I needed help. Miraculously, I made the trip without incident. This was one of the two cars I have owned that I really wish I had kept and never sold.

Demountable Rims

The following illustration shows a demountable rim and the wheel onto which the rim was bolted. The tire, inner tube, and flap were installed on the demountable rim and stayed in place by the air pressure in the tire and inner tube. The rim, with the tire, inner tube, and flap installed, was then installed on the wheel. A hole that was drilled in the rim accommodated the valve in the inner tube. That hole is clearly visible about halfway up the rim. A hole was also drilled in the outer part of the wheel, called a "felloe," to also accommodate the vale in the inner tube. The rim could be bolted onto the wheel only with the two holes for

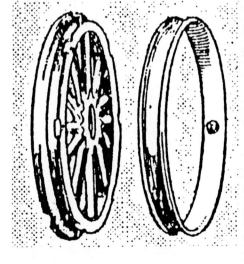

Drawing shows how demountable rim, onto which the tire and inner tube, etc., are installed, can be removed without disturbing the wheel.

Unseen dangers crouch behind a clouded windshield!

the inner tube valve aligned. The easiest way to accomplish this was to rotate the wheel until the hole was at the top of the wheel, then get the hole, with the valve, on the rim at the top as well, and then raise the rim/tire off the ground slightly so that the valve would easily slip into place.

The wheel shown here is a wooden (artillery) wheel, but some automobile makers furnished disc wheels with demountable rims. This 1923 Dodge Brothers as well as the 1923 Lincoln and the 1921 Ford had demountable rims on wooden wheels; the 1929 Chevrolet had demountable rims on disc wheels.

Possibly the reason the tires were so bad was that the correct size (33 × 4) tires were no longer being made. After World War II ended in 1945 Firestone made several antique sizes using its original molds with "nonskid" in the tread. The nearest size available from Firestone was 34 × 4½ which was oversize, but was still 25 inches in diameter and would fit the Dodge Brothers rims. A few years later Firestone and a few other tire makers produced 33 × 4s for those antiques using them as original equipment. They are still available today.

When the rear of the body was cut apart many years earlier, the brackets that held the top when it was folded down were also removed for some unknown reason. Had they been left in place they would not have been in anyone's way. The top appeared to me to be the original one with the car and had not been folded down for many years, if ever.

Early 1920s Outlook

One of the most popular windshield wipers of its time was the clamp-on type. It attached to the top edge of the open car windshield frame and worked from the inside. The driver would move the handle, and the wiper would clean a semicircular area directly in front of the driver's eyes. This is shown in the illustration of a Dodge Brothers open car. All the cars visible with the side curtains in place are Dodge Brothers cars.

6 · *1923 Lincoln*

In the spring of 1950 I saw an ad in the Sunday newspaper for a 1923 Lincoln seven-passenger touring car. I called and drove across town to see it. I was driving my 1925 Dodge Brothers roadster (#3), which made a presentable appearance, even with the side curtains in place. The owner of the Lincoln was a priest and a teacher at the Catholic high school on that side of the city. The original top and upholstery had recently been replaced, but red leather had been used on the seats, and a darker shade of red had been used for the top. Both had been beautifully done. The jump seats still had the original black leather. The fenders, aprons, radiator shell, and shutters appeared to be the original black, with only fair paint. The aluminum body had been brush-painted dark blue, and the nickel plating was thin.

The 17,000 miles showing on the odometer appeared to be correct. The owner said he was certain the mileage was correct. He said he was willed the car by the family of someone who was always one step ahead of the police, who could never get a conviction on him. The owner told me that several of his high school students wanted the car and would have gladly paid his $250.00 asking price, but he feared they were not used to the different quick steering and the odd two-wheel brakes. He also told me that he was impressed that I already had a car of approximately that age and obviously knew how to handle its limitations.

The car had four high-tread, 33 × 5 General tires, a "fat man" steering wheel which would fold part way to make driver entrance and exit easier. Driving was not affected when the steering wheel was locked back in place. The cigarette lighter was mounted on the dash and had a cord on a reel to reach all the way to the back seat. Only one spare

Top: The author and his 1923 Lincoln touring car.
Bottom: Side view of author's 1923 Lincoln giving an idea how long this car was.

tire and rim were with the car although it came equipped to hold two spares. The exiting spare was rather old and very dry.

This Lincoln had been designed by Henry M. Leland and his team, formerly of Cadillac. In 1902 Leland was instrumental in getting Cadillac established, although Olds, Dodge, Ford and Cadillac histories were intertwined in 1902 and 1903. When it became obvious that the United States would be drawn into World War I in 1917, Leland asked the head of General Motors to tool up to build Liberty airplane engines for the country as we had no airplane-building facilities. Leland was told "no." He and many Cadillac executives, designers, engineers, and so on resigned and started the Lincoln Motor Company and built the airplane engines. After World War I ended and there was no more need for large numbers of airplane engines, they decided to build the Lincoln automobile. The first one was produced in 1921. A big U.S. tax mistake caused receivership, and Henry Ford bought Lincoln in 1922.

This car rode very smoothly; Houdaille shock absorbers were standard equipment, and the springs were very long with extremely thin leaves. Also, the gearshift travel was extremely short and easy to use. The car drove and handled very well, and the entire car was "tight." Without my asking, the owner reduced his asking price from $250.00 to $180.00 so that I could get the brush paint redone.

I had made a mental note to replace the dry spare tire as soon as I could. One day I pulled into a gas station, bought my gas and checked the tires. The spare was low so I filled it. Several miles from the gas station was a rough railroad crossing; I knew it was there, so I slowed down as I approached it. As I crossed the tracks I heard a loud bang, like a tire blowing out; the car kept driving properly, however. Nevertheless I stopped and walked around the car, but the tires were fine. Then I checked the spare. It had blown out!

Eventually I located a pair of good 33 × 5, high-tread tires and one extra rim and flap and inner tube. I cleaned and painted the rim I had just purchased as well as the other five rims so they all looked nice and fresh and matched. I put the best Generals on the front and the worst ones on the dual spares and the newly purchased tires on the rear. Matched dual spares gave the car a much more distinguished look than a single spare, especially on a car designed to carry two spares.

I knew that the original vacuum tank no longer worked and that there was an Autopulse electric fuel pump under the hood. Since the 1925 Dodge Brothers Stewart Warner electric fuel pump was working properly, I did not foresee problems with the Autopulse. To my dismay, the Lincoln fuel pump lasted only about three months.

This car went into storage with the others while I was away in the Army. When I returned, the only problem was a dead battery. It was one of the long narrow type, the same type General Motors used on several of its Buick, Oldsmobile, and Pontiac models of the late 1930s to the late 1950s. It was mounted just inside the running board, beside the side apron. An opening was made in the side apron, and a cover concealed the battery.

This car was rather hard to start when cold, and I presumed that caused too much strain on the electric fuel pump. Other people said that I needed a second fuel pump mounted near the gas tank since this car had such a long wheelbase. Someone else said to try a Stewart Warner pump mounted about halfway between the gas tank and the original carburetor. I made a compression test and found that the cylinders were quite uneven on both banks. A fellow with proper valve-grinding equipment and stones helped me grind the valves. I located a pair of new head gaskets and the necessary valves (used) and got the engine running properly.

The valve job did not get finished until the summer of 1952. The car stated right up and ran very well. I had planned to drive it to an old car show about 135 miles away. A day or two beforehand I had noticed that the engine was overheating. Since I had had the radiator cleaned out as part of the valve-grinding procedure as a precaution, I didn't understand the overheating after a superficial look for a leak or something else obvious. What I didn't realize was that the timing chain had jumped a notch or two.

I started off late Friday morning for the 135-mile drive to the car show, expecting to arrive a few hours later. Somewhere I made a wrong turn, in addition to having to stop several times due to overheating. Eventually I found the right road to the car show. Once, when I let my foot up off the accelerator there was a "pop" noise, and the engine quit running. I coasted off the road and tried to restart the engine. It just spun over freely as if there were no resistance. In fact there was indeed no resistance since the timing chain had jumped a few more notches and the valves were no longer opening and closing at the right time to make compression. I was able to get a ride back home, arriving very late. Early the next morning I was able to borrow a pickup truck and a long piece of chain. I solicited my brother's reluctant help, and we dragged the Lincoln back to my rented garage.

By this time the odometer showed 22,000 miles. After removing the timing chain I laid it on a flat surface and was able to push it against itself, then pull it back and discovered close to half an inch of play. I have never figured out why a high-quality car with such low mileage would have a timing chain stretched so badly. I have never heard, before or since, of another Lincoln of this era having a timing chain stretch like this one did. I was unable to locate other gears or a chain, so I advertised the car for sale. By the time I found a buyer in early 1953 I had sold the 1925 Dodge Brothers roadster (#3) and the 1923 Dodge Brothers touring car (#4) and had bought and sold #7 and #8. This car was not sold outright but was traded for cash and a 1917 Dodge Brothers touring car in need of restoration.

The trade was made with a fellow in southern Minnesota. Part of the deal was that I would deliver the Lincoln to him and pick up the trade and the rest of the money. I rented a 1952 Dodge truck, cab over engine, with a bed long enough to accommodate the long-wheelbase Lincoln. I knew of a gas station with an outside drive-on lift, so, again with my brother's help, we towed the Lincoln there, muscled it onto the lift, raised the lift to the height of the truck bed and rolled the Lincoln on. We then securely blocked and tied it down.

I made the three-day trip to Minnesota alone. The truck over-heated about one hundred miles from home. Fortunately, I was able to get to a garage about half a mile away, where they found that the head gasket had blown. The truck had a flathead, six-cylinder engine. When the garage mechanics removed the cylinder head they found it too badly warped to plane down smooth. That meant getting a new cylinder head. The biggest delay was the several-hour wait for the new head to be delivered. The rest of the trip was made without incident.

When I returned the rental truck the expense of the cylinder head breakdown was deducted without question. I had brought the warped head back with me for them to do with as they saw fit.

Many high-end car makers produced seven-passenger touring cars during the 1910s and 1920s; in the late 1920s these became even fancier and were known as phaetons. Even during the 1930s enclosed seven-passenger sedans could be ordered from several manufacturers. To make a seven-passenger car, the manufacturer merely had to extend the frame and chassis of a five-passenger car and then add two extra folding seats. The two extra seats folded flat against the back of the front seat when not in use. The regular rear seat was not disturbed. Three people sat in the regular rear seat, then the two jump seats were folded out and one person sat in each one. These, with two people in the front seat, accounted for seven passengers.

The Lincoln had what was nicknamed a "fat man's" steering wheel because it could slip up out of the way to give a large man more room to get behind the wheel. It was designed to lock in the steering position before the car could be driven. The car's front wheels had to be pointing straight ahead before the wheel could be moved out of the way. Several U.S. car makers offered fat man steering wheels as standard equipment or accessories during the 1910s and 1920s.

The author's 1923 Lincoln as it arrived in Minnesota for the trade.

With the advent of adjustable front seats in the late 1920s, these steering wheels were no longer needed.

The one on my 1923 Lincoln worked a little differently from the one shown opposite. It folded flat, down against the steering column, instead of sliding up as this one did. Pulling the Lincoln steering wheel back to its driving position clicked it into place. The car could not be driven with the steering wheel folded down.

Lincoln Engine

The following illustration shows the Lincoln engine, always a V-8 until the early 1930s. As was the technology at the time, each cylinder block was bolted to the crank case. Lincoln's chief competitor, Cadillac, made its engine with the "V" at a 90 degree angle. Lincoln made its engine with a 60 degree angle. Each was convinced that its

Plenty
of
Room

No trouble to get in or out of your car if it is equipped with a Neville More-Room Steering Wheel. Just push it up out of the way and walk in or out with *ease.*

Adds as much to your car in value and appearance as it does in comfort. Handsomely made of black walnut and polished aluminum. Standard equipment on many of America's finest cars. Made for every make. Ask your auto dealer today.

Neville Steering Wheel & Mfg. Co.
WAYNE   -:-   MICHIGAN

Ad shows how fat man steering wheel moves out of the way. The advent of adjustable front seats made these obsolete.

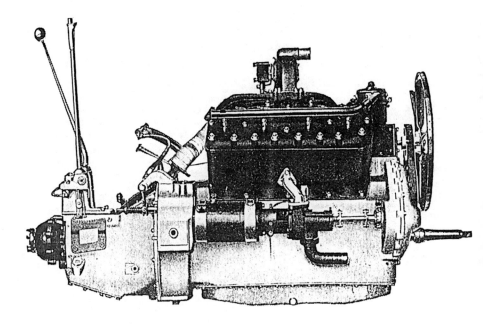

Lincoln V-8 engine and transmission assembly of the 1920s.

design was the best. A lot of people do not realize that the Cadillac and Lincoln companies were both started by the same man.

This car had a huge, motor-driven ooga horn, which had a deep throaty tone, not a squawk like the sound of the horn of a low-priced car. The ooga horn was mounted on the right side of the cowl just above the toe board. The motor part of the horn was inside the car, and the bell, or trumpet, of the horn was under the hood on the right side. It was held in place by about a dozen bolts because it was so big. Other cars of this era usually had the horn somewhere on the engine.

Several makes of U.S. cars in the 1910s and 1920s did not have a dip stick to check the engine oil. Instead, each had a float-type gauge. This Lincoln had such a gauge. There was a pointer on the left side of the outside of the engine. The float would cause the pointer to indicate whether oil was needed.

The 1917, 1923, and 1925 Dodge Brothers cars I had all used the same style float oil gauge. There was a small hole in the left side of the engine block between #1 and #2 cylinders. A thin rod went through this hole to a float inside the engine's crank case. When the rod protruded about two inches above the engine block, all was well; about one inch above the block meant that it was a quart low. When barely visible, oil was needed immediately. By the late 1920s every U.S. auto manufacturer had switched to the more accurate dip sticks.

When car makers realized that headlights could glare into the eyes of oncoming drivers, Lincoln developed a unique way of handling this situation. The company made the headlight reflectors able to dip up or down. A handle for this was located on the left side of the steering column. When it was flipped up, there was a series of rods and levers connecting the handle with each headlight reflector to tip it up for night driving or dip down for regular city driving at night. This mechanical system was the best one available until the advent of the electrically operated dimmer switch, first made available in the early 1930s.

7 • *1942 Chevrolet*

This car came to me from the original owner, a company, but I was able to keep it for only about three months. In September 1950 the company where I had been working decided to replace three or four of its automobiles, one of which was this 1942 Chevrolet two-door. It was strictly a "nothing" car as far as I was concerned, but at the time the only other cars I had were the 1925 Dodge Brothers roadster, the 1923 Dodge Brothers touring car and the 1923 Lincoln touring car. At least this was a more modern car with a good heater and defroster.

The car was a "blackout," meaning that it was assembled between the second week of December 1941 and the second week of February 1942, when civilian auto production was halted. The only chrome on the car was on the bumpers and guards because those parts had already been stockpiled by the second week of December 1941, when additional chrome production was halted for the war effort (World War II). Chromium was considered a precious metal and had to be imported. The government thought that chrome could be put to better use than decorating automobiles. All U.S. auto makers made blackout models during those weeks, not just Chevrolet. This particular 1942 Chevrolet was dark blue, and the normally chrome-plated parts were painted yellow.

The first year that the entire GM line of cars had the fenders extending into the doors was 1942. There were sheet metal "caps" on the doors to extend the look of the rear of the fenders. Some of the very expensive 1940 and 1941 Cadillac models had these caps. The 1942 Chevrolet had the same basic body style as the 1941 model; the biggest difference was the grille, the hood, and the above mentioned fenders with the caps extending on the doors.

Mechanically, the 1942 models were basically a carryover from the 1941 and earlier Chevrolets. One of the carryover features was a vacuum-assisted gearshift that was supposed to ease the shift lever to actually shift the gears inside the transmission. It worked reasonably well. And if it failed to work properly you could still drive the car and shift in the normal way; it was just a little harder.

I had also worked for this company as an errand boy during high school, and I remember when they took delivery on it. The company had to get a "priority" from the ration board after proving that the car was needed to keep the company going; a priority for the spare tire was also needed. As well as I can recall, the company actually got the car in late 1942 or early 1943. I knew that it had always been well maintained and had never been wrecked or abused. Since this was a company car it did not have a radio. The only accessory was the heater/defroster package.

When the company bought this car during World War II no one knew how long it was going to have to last. Before placing this car in service the company sent it to an auto upholstery shop and had the door and quarter-panel upholstery panels removed and covered with red leatherette. The original factory upholstery was left there, and the leatherette was installed over it. The idea was that the leatherette could be removed later to reveal the unused factory upholstery at trade-in time. This company had done this to a few of its other late-model cars also. When I bought this car the leatherette was still there and still looked very good, so I left it alone.

After this car had been in service a couple of years, sometime in 1944 or 1945, it was in a minor accident while parked. The person to whom the car was assigned was away from the car to make a phone call. On returning to the car, the driver saw that the grille was pushed in. There was no damage to anything but the grille and the center vertical grille bar. Since there was no other damage and the running of the car was not impaired and new parts were not available, no attempt was made to repair it. In late 1945, when government restrictions had been lifted, new grilles in primer paint became available. The company had the grille replaced but for some reason did not have it painted; it was left in gray primer. The center vertical grille bar was not replaced, and the body man merely pounded it out enough to reinstall, making no attempt to get it to fit properly. Although the damaged grille was replaced, the replacement did not look any better than the damaged one.

Had I been able to keep this car I would have removed the grille and had it painted right and bought a new vertical grille bar and had it painted, too.

The reason I had this car for only three months is that in early December I learned that I was going to be drafted in early January. When I told my supervisor at the company that I was to be drafted, he let me know that he expected me to sell the car to him for what I had paid for it. That wasn't what I had wanted to happen, but rather than argue I agreed. I had not put any money into the car other than tuning the engine.

Through others in the company whom I knew I learned that my former supervisor kept the car for a couple of years, then traded it in for a new 1952 Chevrolet, the cheapest black two-door sedan with no accessories. Later he had a heater, a defroster, and an oil filter installed.

One flaw in every 1941 Chevrolet was that the lower part of the cowl rusted through between the back of the front fender and the front of the front door. Every 1941 Chevrolet I have seen either had been repaired or was due to be repaired where it had rusted through. Since the 1942 and subsequent models had the fenders extending back to the door cap, no rust was visible.

Because 1942 models were produced for just a few months, they were a bit unusual, whether a Chevrolet or another make of 1942 car. Police departments had good reason to replace their units when they were beyond repair after being badly burned or wrecked. When a priority was obtained for a new police car it was usually a coupe. The red flashing light and siren combination was mounted on top of the left front fender. When World War II ended and the police departments replaced their 1942 cars, it was impossible to completely hide where the red light and siren combination had been removed and the front fender patched. The cars wound up on used car lots usually for lower prices because no one wanted an ex-police car that most likely needed rebuilding of all of its mechanical units.

8 · 1939 Plymouth

After my honorable discharge from the army in May 1951, I needed a reliable modern car. I found a 1939 Plymouth three-passenger coupe; it was the deluxe model with the gearshift on the steering column. For Plymouth 1939 was sort of an interim year. It was the third year for the same basic body style. The 1938s had been a facelift of the 1937s. For 1939 the grille, hood, and front fenders were quite different. The headlights were mounted in the outer edges of the front fenders for the first time. Prior to 1939 the headlights had been mounted on the sides of the grilles and slightly above the fenders. Now, for 1939, the headlights were square! Not just for Plymouth, but for all Chrysler-made automobiles.

That style last for only one year, however, as the 1940 models of all U.S.-built automobiles introduced the much better "sealed beam" headlights. Different after-market companies made kits for 1939 and older cars to convert those cars to sealed beams. My 1939 Plymouth had been converted when I found it. It had been repainted the original dark gray a few years earlier. The sealed beam conversion kit was painted the same color so it must have been converted before the paint job.

I found my car on a small used-car lot. The paint was quite dull so I washed the car thoroughly, applied Simoniz cleaner and then Simoniz paste wax. I put it on nice and thick. At least once a week I wiped it dry with a clean, dry cotton rag. It seemed to shine more with each dry wipedown; by the end of three or four months it really glistened.

This was also the last year for the windshield wipers to be on top of the windshield on Plymouths. For the 1940 models the wipers pivoted on the bottom of each windshield glass and cleaned a much larger area of glass in front of the driver and passenger. In 1939 Plymouth first came out with a two-piece windshield. It had a chrome divider strip down the middle, and the glass on each side was swept back for stream-lining.

That year was the first time that the gearshift on the steering col-umn was available on the higher-priced Plymouths only. The low-priced Plymouth, the Roadking, and also the lowest-priced Chevrolet and Ford models still had the gearshift on the floor, the same as prior models. Cadillac had the gearshift on the steering column ("three on the three") on its expensive models in 1938. Oldsmobile and Buick had the controls of their automatic safety transmission mounted just below the steering wheel in 1937 and 1938. Hudson also had its "electric hand" control mounted just under the steering wheel. Those were available on the most expensive models only.

I had this car about eight months. I really wanted a four-door sedan but took this 1939 Plymouth coupe because it was available and ran well at a price that I could afford. Then I found #9.

This car performed flawlessly the entire time I owned it. The only work I did on it was the Simonizing.

This was the first model year that Plymouth and the rest of the Chrysler cars had an unusual lighted speedometer. The company referred to it as its "safety speedometer." When these cars were driven with any of the lights on, the speedometer light would be green when moving below 35 miles an hour; from 35 to 50 miles an hour it would be yellow, and above 50 miles an hour it would be red. This feature was kept for ten model years, through the early 1949 models even though the speedometer styling was changed several times on the different brands of Chrysler cars several times. Technically only seven model years were involved because no new civilian passenger cars were made for the 1943, 1944 and 1945 model years and only a relatively few for the 1942 model run.

Like every other three-passenger coupe made by all U.S. auto makers from the mid-1930s through 1948, this one was beautifully streamlined. A three-passenger coupe has only a front seat, which, the-oretically, could hold three people. By its nature the trunk was cav-ernous, tapering gracefully down from the slanted rear window to the rear bumper.

In an attempt to achieve a more streamlined effect, the 1939 Ply-mouth taillights were changed from the 1938 and previous year models' beautiful teardrop shape on each rear fender to merely a red lens with a rear-pointing reflector right on the rear portion of the fender itself. The bulb, socket, and so on were below the surface of the fender but, since the light fixture was mounted low on the fender, it could be seen from the rear at night. The only problem was that the light assembly was mounted directly behind the wheel and rusted out fairly quickly from water, dirt, and so forth being thrown up by the rear tires. For its 1940 and later models Plymouth and the rest of the Chrysler Corporation cars had completely new bodies with taillights that were much larger and were mounted on the rear body panel between the trunk and rear fender, away from any possibility of rusting out.

9 · *1941 Dodge*

Another used-car lot is where I found a 1941 Dodge four-door sedan with fluid drive. It ran beautifully and had the original very shiny black paint and a rebuilt engine. Whoever switched the rebuilt with the original engine did not use the correct engine mounts or something as the bell housing on the rear of the engine would touch the underside of the floor under certain conditions and cause an annoying vibration. Locating the problem took more time then fixing it.

All that was required to fix it was to take a big hammer and apply it sharply to the underside of the metal floor pan several times in exactly the right locations. When I first got the car it had a slight miss only at high speeds. Replacing the spark plugs corrected that problem. I also tested the compression while the spark plugs were out and learned that everything inside the engine was fine. As a precaution I also replaced the spark plug wires, distributor cap, rotor, points and condenser.

Besides the factory radio and heater/defroster, this car also had built-in turn signals, which also included the big front parking lights mounted on the tops of each fender. Turn signals were accessories on all but the most expensive cars in 1941. Although electric signals with switch and flasher are taken for granted nowadays, the driver at the time was required to roll down his window, in every kind of weather, and put his hand and arm outside to signal. Straight out meant a left turn; pointing up meant a right turn; forearm down meant slow or stop. Although signaling was legally required many drivers neglected to do so.

Many aftermarket companies made kits consisting of the switch (to be installed on the left side of the steering post) along with necessary wiring, flasher, and double contact sockets with double contact bulbs. This kit would connect the parking lights to give the car front turn signals and connect the brake lights to give the car rear turn signals. Electric turn signals were not legally required as factory equipment in some states until the 1955 models.

The big accessory front and rear bumper/grille guards were lying in the trunk when I got the car. The special bolts needed to hold them in place were bent and twisted, but not the guards themselves. I went to a dealer and bought the correct new bolts and hardware and I installed them; this made the car look the way it should have looked in addition to giving the protection of the guards.

This car was a dream to drive, but I just could not afford the gasoline required by the fluid drive. Fluid drive was available on some 1940 model Chryslers with the straight-eight engine, then on all 1941 Chrysler and DeSoto cars with the semiautomatic transmission and on all 1941 Dodges with standard gearshift. A lot of people are not aware that fluid drive was invented in England by the Lanchester Motor Car Company. The Chrysler Corporation decided to use it and, per an agreement with Lanchester, paid that company a royalty fee for every Dodge, DeSoto and Chrysler car using fluid drive. After about six months I could no longer afford the gasoline it consumed, so I sold it and bought #10. Had I known how relatively cheap it was to have the fluid drive removed, I would have done so and kept the regular standard transmission.

Although I would eventually own more than two dozen cars with rotary door latches, this was the first car I owned that was actually equipped with them. Chrysler introduced them on its 1940 models and eventually the rest of the industry had various versions of rotary door latches. This type of latch was easy to operate and very positive acting, and the doors would close all the way without slamming. The outside door handles on all U.S.-built cars had been the twist-down type since the late teens and continued to be so until the late 1940s.

Another unusual feature of all Chrysler cars of the 1940 through the early 1949 models was the trunk lid. It was a compound steel unit, curving from top to bottom and also from right to left. The previous models from the mid-1930s through the 1939s were curved top to bottom. Likewise, the late 1949 and subsequent models also had the basic top-to-bottom curve only.

10 · 1936 Dodge

This car was a 1936 Dodge three-passenger coupe, the higher-priced model with two windshield wipers, two taillights, two horns, and beauty rings on the wheels. An add-on accessory was the radio, but it did not need the outside aerial that it actually had as it came factory equipped with a built-in aerial in the roof chicken wire. This was the last year for the cloth insert roof, and chicken wire was a layer below the outer covering. The car had a standard aerial connection that came down inside the left windshield post with the connector plug between the door post and the steering column, below the dash board. Whoever installed this radio apparently did not know this and installed an outside aerial on the left cowl. The reception was better with the roof aerial.

Another add-on accessory was a Southwind gasoline heater. As soon as I learned how to use it correctly I really enjoyed it. It would absolutely run you out of that car on even the coldest day! I learned to shut the heater off about two miles before turning off the engine. By doing this the heater would keep on running until all the gasoline inside the heater and feed pipes was all used up; only then would it shut off.

By that time I was only a couple of blocks from my destination. People who did not shut the heater off ahead of time always had trouble with them because of the carbon from the unburned gasoline lying inside the heater. About once a month during cold weather I would fill the gas tank with ethyl gasoline to keep the heater clean. More than once a gas station attendant (in the days of self-service only) would ask me why I wanted such expensive gas in such an old car. My reply was always "To keep the gasoline heater clean." Each one would look at me as if I were crazy (a charge I have never denied).

The author's 1936 Dodge three-passenger coupe.

Around 1959 Chrysler equipped some of its big cars with gasoline heaters. I think they were most often found in the DeSoto line, but some medium Chryslers also had them. Owners would not shut them off early, and eventually the unburned gasoline still in the heater would backfire, frightening everyone. Usually the heater would not work again until cleaned out. As far as I can recall these cars had gasoline heaters for only one or two model years.

Shortly after I got this car I found four high-tread, take-off white sidewall 6.00 × 16 tires for $20.00. They really set off the dark blue car. As with all three-passenger coupes, the trunk was huge. The spare tire was stored upright behind the passenger seat back, allowing even more room in the trunk.

One near-major problem occurred with this 1936 Dodge, but I caught it before it became major. Had I not recognized it and had it fixed immediately, it would have been a very expensive repair. On the way home from work one evening I heard a strange noise in second gear. It sounded like the metal shield on one of the ball bearings inside the transmission had come loose. I continued on home, then went back to work the next morning avoiding second gear as much as possible. I left the car with a mechanic I knew close to where I worked.

He confirmed my suspicion, saying that the shield would have become wedged between the gears, chewing up everything in sight if it had come completely off the bearing. He asked me if the clutch was okay as with the transmission already out this would be the ideal time to replace the clutch. I told him that it was fine. When I picked up the car he told me that he had replaced all the all bearings inside the transmission as well as the needle bearings as they were showing signs of wear.

Another time, without my realizing it until it happened, the car's cylinder head blew a head gasket. Where it blew, on the engine, was not a place where water would leak into a cylinder, so it was no more than inconvenient, noisy, and sluggish. All these Chrysler flathead six-cylinder engines had a capillary tube screwed into a fitting on the left side of the cylinder head for the heat gauge on the dashboard. Often these became stuck and would not unscrew, resulting in a broken heat gauge. I had to drive the car with the blown head gasket for a couple of days before I was able to replace it. To avoid possible problems I put penetrating oil on the heat gauge fitting a couple of times. When I finally replaced the head gasket, the heat gauge fitting unscrewed fairly easily.

After a while I noticed that the seat was no longer comfortable. I found a set of seat covers and a couple of pillows. I put one pillow on the back rest and the other on the seat cushion, then put the seat cover over each. This took care of the problem as long as I kept the car.

Until its 1940 models the Chrysler Corporation made some of its cars with the windshield wipers pivoting from the top of the windshield. The DeSoto and Chrysler cars had wipers pivoting on the bottom of the windshield a few years earlier. In the bottom-pivoting type, one motor was used, and it was located under the center of the dashboard with the arms to the wiper pivots the same length on each side. Both wipers were required to keep the system in balance.

On the lower-priced Plymouths (and Dodges), where the wipers pivoted above the windshield, all had one wiper for the left as standard equipment. The wiper motor was vacuum operated, located above the windshield, and actuated by an on/off, push/pull switch. When a new car customer ordered a wiper for the right side as well, all the dealer mechanic had to do was to remove the inside windshield garnish molding, then partly lower the headliner upholstery to add the right wiper motor. The roof metal had the mounting brackets already welded in at the factory, where it was more practical to do so. The mechanic was given a template, so he would drill the hole in the roof in exactly the right place for the pivot shaft to go through. A length of vacuum tubing was run from the existing left wiper motor over to the right side. A vacuum "tee" was added to the line to supply engine vacuum to each motor. The mechanic then reinstalled the headliner and the garnish molding and installed the switch on the inside and the wiper arm and blade on the outside.

The right wiper motor was different from the left one so it would park with the arm and blade to the outside. Each wiper motor was turned on and off separately although there wasn't much reason to use the right one by itself. Ford and General Motors were also changing their various models.

After about two years the time was approaching when I was going to have to spend considerable money for normal wear items, such as brakes, seals, wheel cylinders, and tires. I decided to look for a later-model car and found #12.

A previous owner of this car had replaced the original headlight parts with a sealed beam conversion kit. It appeared to have been professionally done by a good mechanic because everything fit properly and worked just fine as long as I had the car.

Beginning in the mid-1930s Chrysler began equipping all its cars with oval-shaped brake and clutch pedal pads, either brown or black, to match the floor mat. When the rubber on the pads wore down in normal use, they could easily be replaced. Plymouth and Dodge cars had these into the mid-1950s; DeSoto and Chrysler had them until the fluid drive years. Although the cars left the assembly plant with the pedals in the vertical position, several people I knew did as I did and turned them to the horizontal position, merely by loosening the retaining nut on the back of the pedal and rotating the pad a quarter turn, then tightening the nut — about a thirty-second job. I found them to be easier to operate that way.

11 · *1917 Dodge Brothers*

Early in 1953 I acquired a 1917 Dodge Brothers touring car in a very unrestored condition but just about complete. I had given the 1923 Lincoln (still apart with the stretched timing chain) and received the 1917 Dodge Brothers and some cash. One of the few missing items was the six-blade fan, but I was able to locate a good one, used. The fan belt was the original flat leather type and looked like the original belt. Getting the engine to run was a simple matter of buying a twelve-volt battery, still somewhat unusual in 1953, making up and installing the five wires to the distributor cap from the spark plugs and coil, and priming the carburetor with gasoline. The vacuum tank worked as long as I had the car.

On one of my early trips under the car I noticed that where the aluminum engine crank case bolted up to the frame engine mount, one of the mounts had broken off and a steel support had been fabricated and installed in its place. Since the repair appeared to have been professionally done and had been holding for many, many years, I let well enough alone. I had no trouble with it as long as I had the car.

A rather time-consuming problem turned out to be the brakes; they would drag all the time. A very careful inspection under the car revealed the problem: The two left brake rods, for both the foot and hand brake, were badly bowed. It appeared that the car had run over a large rock or something. There was no damage to any other part of the car. The complete left rear wheel and the whole brake mechanism, including the full floating-axle shaft, had to be removed for access to each rod. Then each rod had to have two operating levers removed from each woodruff key. A good mechanic I knew was able to

The author's 1917 Dodge Brothers touring car shortly after returning from Minnesota. Everything had been painted orange. The "Courtland F.D." had used the car in a parade in Courtland, Minnesota, several years earlier. The car had just been put in running condition.

straighten each rod properly. Reassembly went a lot faster; end of brake problem.

This car's serial number indicated that it went along the final assembly line in Detroit in April 1917, just as the United States was entering "the war to end all wars." The two Dodge brothers had been building cars since late 1914, known as 1915 models. For ten years the Dodge Brothers machine shop in Detroit built the mechanical parts for the Ford Motor Company. In 1913 these two companies decided to go their separate ways, Ford building its own foundries and so on and the Dodges building a car with all the improvements they thought Ford should have been making all along. The very early Dodge Brothers cars had magneto ignition instead of distributors and also cone clutches instead of the more modern multiple-disc clutches.

The Budd company made all-steel bodies instead of bodies made of wood with sheet metal panels nailed onto the outside and upholstery tacked onto the inside. The Dodges saw the value of all-steel bodies because they were so much stronger in addition to being free from squeaks and rattles.

Top: The author's 1917 Dodge Brothers just after the body, hood, and radiator shell had been painted with the fenders, aprons, and so on removed. The fenders and aprons were painted while still off the car and then reinstalled.

Bottom: The author's car "after."

The author's car "after." The top should have had six little windows in the back instead of five, but the rest of the top was so beautifully made, the author did not complain to the top installer. No comments were ever made, so probably no one who saw the car realized this minor omission. These were called "cathedral" windows.

The JOHNSON
SHOCK ABSORBER

The only coil spring shock absorber with a recoil check

When anyone talks shock absorbers to you, ask to see the inside of the case. It's the shock absorber exposed that tells the story. Other coil spring shock absorbers are not founded upon the sound engineering principles of the Johnson and therefore cannot afford Johnson qualities.

The coil on the end of a spring acts in the same relation that a pneumatic tire does to a wheel, takes the shock that automobile springs cannot absorb. Acts with every move of the spring softening and cushioning its action. The Johnsons are easily attached to rear springs of any car with semi or three-quarter full-elliptic design.

Engineers pronounce the coil spring the most effective for shock absorption. But a single-spring absorber is helpless against the rebound. The Johnson has two springs and the inner spring smothers this recoil. It is this mechanical difference that makes the Johnson so superior to the ordinary kind. They are actually doubly effective.

Note carefully the illustration of the Johnson exposed.

Note the four struss rods, made of $\frac{7}{16}$ cold rolled steel.

Note the steel spring cup for the inner coil.

This construction is trouble-proof and break-proof.

The four struss rods, made of $\frac{7}{16}$ cold rolled steel, which carry the load, pass through four machined holes in the top cap and fasten into the hanger heads, as shown in cut, making this absorber water and dust proof. These rods connect to compression plate, in which the large or outer coil rests, the light or inside coil resting in spring cup, carried on top of larger coil, which gives a tandem movement of the spring or graduated tension. The small or inner coil carrying the light load, or taking up the light jars and when the tension of this small coil is compressed to equal the tension of the outer coil, the outer coil then takes up the jars allowing the spring cup to pass through the bottom compression plate, giving a long free action of over 2 inches and when the inside coil is fully compressed it then acts as a check to the rebound of the car.

In ordering give make, model and year of car.

PRICES PER PAIR

Junior type for all pleasure cars with ¾ Elliptic Springs weighing less than 2200 lbs.....$12.00
For pleasure cars weighing less than 3500 lbs... 16.87
Heavy type for cars weighing 3500 lbs. and more... 22.50
Extra heavy type for commercial Trucks.. 30.00

The type of spring-loaded shock absorbers installed as accessories on the rear springs of the author's 1917 Dodge Brothers.

BRAKE BAND TOP SUPPORT

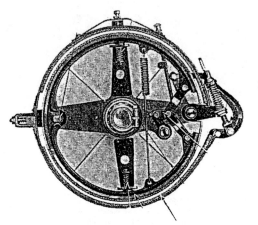

FRONT OF CAR ⟶
OPERATING LEVER

BRAKE BAND
REAR SUPPORT

BRAKE BAND WITH LINING

Typical mechanically operated brake system of the teens and 1920s. Right rear is shown.

The brake mechanism shown here is for the right (rear) brake on a car with two wheel brakes. This particular illustration is of a Dodge Brothers from 1915 through 1927. Until the mid 1920s almost all U.S.-built cars used this same basic brake system. In this drawing, the brake drum has been removed. The foot operated on the outside of the brake drum by squeezing (contracting) it. The emergency brake operated on the inside of the brake drum by expanding.

The "brake band rear support" kept the outside band section of the brake band rigid, as did the "brake band top support." Each one could be adjusted (with the wheel removed). There was a rod connecting the top side of the operating lever (not shown in the illustration). When the driver stepped on the brake pedal the operating lever moved toward the front of the car through a series of levers as shown here, causing the brake band to squeeze against the brake drum, which was bolted to the wheel, to stop the wheel from revolving.

In 1917 the wheelbase of the cars was increased from the original 110" wheelbase to a 114" wheelbase. This car was among the first to have the 114" wheelbase.

In what turned out to be a rehearsal for World War I, an experiment was made by Lieutenant George Patton, a young cavalry officer at the time. He would later become very famous as a World War II gen-

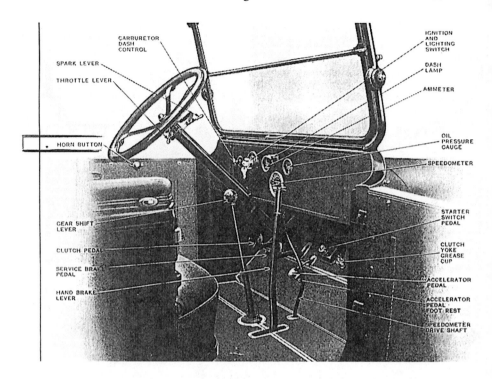

CARBURETOR
DASH
CONTROL

SPARK LEVER

THROTTLE LEVER

IGNITION
AND
LIGHTING
SWITCH

DASH
LAMP

AMMETER

HORN BUTTON

OIL
PRESSURE
GAUGE

SPEEDOMETER

GEAR SHIFT
LEVER

CLUTCH PEDAL

SERVICE BRAKE
PEDAL

HAND BRAKE
LEVER

STARTER
SWITCH
PEDAL

CLUTCH
YOKE
GREASE
CUP

ACCELERATOR
PEDAL

ACCELERATOR
PEDAL
FOOT REST

SPEEDOMETER
DRIVE SHAFT

Front compartment.

eral. In 1916 he made a cavalry charge against the Mexican bandit Pancho Villa using Dodge Brothers touring cars!

When horns began to be installed on automobiles, they were placed at the driver's left hand. When cars became equipped with electric lights the plunger device was changed to an electric horn mounted either under the hood or somewhere on the front of the car. The control, an electric push button, was placed near the driver's left hand on the upholstery panel at the top of the left front door. My 1917 Dodge Brothers had the button mounted there. It wasn't until the 1922 models that Dodge Brothers began mounting the horn button in the center of the steering wheel. People would come up to the left side of this car, put their hands on top of the left front door with a finger accidentally on the horn button. The blowing horn would startle everyone around. I solved the problem by changing the horn wire connecting from the ammeter on the dashboard to the live side of the ignition switch; then it would blow only when the horn button was pushed with the ignition key on, which meant that I was driving the car.

This car must have had a high-speed rear axle because a couple of years later a couple in their modern car clocked me at 70 miles an hour on the way to an old car show. When we met at the show they asked me if I knew how fast I had been driving. I told them that the drum-type speedometer registered only as high as 60, but it was showing right around 55. I was very surprised when they told me that I had been going 70. I would never have knowingly driven that car that fast.

Eventually I overhauled the engine in this car; a previous overhaul included a rebore of the cylinders to .020 oversize with oversize pistons and rings. The original ignition coil gave out after thirty-eight years, and I had to replace it with a modern round coil because that was all that was available at the moment. The original flat leather fan belt came apart one weekend while I was out of town. I had to settle for what the nearest gas station had on hand of the proper length. It worked until I could locate the correct replacement.

All Dodge Brothers cars from the 1915 models through the 1923 models had three-quarter elliptic rear springs with a single shackle connecting the two sections at the rear. A previous owner had replaced the original shackles with spring-loaded shock absorbers. Each canister contained a heavy coil spring which hung down beneath the shackle/shock absorber. They were designed to absorb some of the jolts and jounces whereas the standard shackle would just pass them along without absorbing anything. They looked as old as the car so they were probably installed by the original owner. One day a teenaged hot rodder was respectfully looking the car over very carefully. When he walked around to the back of the car and spotted the rear shocks, he exclaimed: "Man, dig those *kah-rayzee* lowering blocks!"

The original tires on all Dodge Brothers touring cars and roadsters of this era were 32 × 3½ smooth tread on the front and 32 × 3 ? tires with tread on the rear and no spare tire or inner tube. A spare rim and the place to mount it, plus tools to change and repair a tire, were included but not the spare itself. All U.S. manufacturers of medium- and low-priced cars were equipped this way, not just Dodge Brothers. Since only the rear wheels had driving and braking power, only the rear tires had tread. All the front wheels did was steer the car so it was thought that tread on them was not needed.

When it came time to replace the tires, most owners replaced the originals with one size larger, 33 × 4, which were smoother riding than the 32 × 3½ original size; they also bought tires with tread for all four tires on the ground as well as for the spare. This is what one of the previous owners had done with this car. The original size of 32 × 3½ is 25 inches in diameter; so is the oversize of 33 × 4. Both fit the rim with no alterations of any kind.

Eventually I removed the fenders, aprons, and so on and had them painted black and the body and hood painted dark blue. The radiator shell was also painted black. This was the era when chrome or nickel-plated radiator shells were reserved for expensive cars, not cars in the Dodge Brothers price range. Finding the right color linoleum for the floor and running boards took some searching but were eventually found, likewise moldings for the borders of the running boards.

Last came the new, light tan top with the exclusive Dodge Brothers cathedral-style rear curtain isinglass windows and a light tan top boot and spare tire cover. The semiretired man who made them made one mistake and that was that he made only five rear-window isinglass lights instead of six as the original had. Everything else he did was so perfect, however, including cutting the rear curve to come down and meet the rear of the body in exactly the right place, that I did not mention the curtain lights to him. That light tan top really set off the rest of the car.

Friends of mine were getting married one Saturday in June. The reception was to begin at 8:00 P.M. in the church hall. I had plans to go to an old car show the next morning about 50 miles away. I attended the wedding in the morning driving my regular car there. Later in the day I put my regular car in the garage I rented for this touring car and took the touring car out to drive it a while to make sure everything was okay for the trip to the old car show on Sunday. Then I drove it home.

My plan was to drive the 1917 touring car to the 8 P.M. reception, arriving about 8:15 or so and park out of the way while it was still daylight. Then I would drive home later (about 5 miles) after dark. When I had the rest of the chrome plating done I also had the headlight reflectors done, so the headlights were now as bright as they had been in 1917. I also added a second taillight, and all the lights were working properly; I was certain that everything would be fine for only 5 miles. My plan was to get an early start Sunday morning right after early church.

For some reason the bride and groom were a little late arriving at the reception and had gone inside the hall just a moment or two before

I arrived. Most of the guests were still outside as I pulled into the parking lot. The car immediately became the center of attention, which is what I had wanted to avoid by arriving fifteen minutes late. Other guests, who knew of my plans, could see my embarrassment. When I went through the reception line to offer my congratulations and best wishes to the newlyweds, they were bubbling over with such happiness that the attention my car had attracted did not diminish the joy of their day.

In early 1958 I sold this car because I had owned it for about five years and had grown tired of it.

This car and all Dodge Brothers touring cars and roadsters made through the 1927 models had a very unusual feature. The Budd Company made the all-steel bodies. The unusual feature was the door hinge design. Any of the doors could be removed merely by opening the door all the way, then lifting it straight up. No tools were required! To reinstall the door one basically reversed the procedure. Care had to be taken not to scratch anything when reinstalling because both pins on the door had to line up *exactly* with both sockets on the body's door post before it could be closed.

Although Dodge Brothers as well as several other U.S. car manufactures did not make specific changes for each year, running changes sometimes coincided with calendar years. One such change was the addition of a U-shaped apron under the radiator and between the front frame horns. It hid the inside of the frame horns as well as the front springs and axle to make a much nicer appearance for the 1917 and later models.

This car, as well as the 1923 Lincoln, #6, had full floating rear axles. Basically, each axle shaft does nothing but make its particular wheel revolve; it carries no weight. A few model years later manufacturers realized that full floating axles were not needed for automobiles and that semifloating ones worked just as well and did not cost as much to manufacture. One unusual feature of those two cars was that the front hub caps were different from the rear ones, so they would not interchange. Hub caps of this era, until the late 1920s, screwed on and off and had a hex shape on the outer edge. A hex-shaped tool came with each car, and its sole purpose was to screw and unscrew the hub caps. The tool would fit the hex fitting on all four wheels, however.

Semifloating rear axles took the same hub cap as the fronts. Then,

Bolan

5959 HOLLYWOOD BLVD., LOS ANGELES 28, CALIF.

HOLLYWOOD 2-3261

September 30, 1957

Mr. Nelson Bolan
709 Glenshire Avenue
Cincinnati 26, Ohio

Dear Mr. Bolan:

We are pleased to inform you that your entry in
Motor Trend's Custom Car Contest has been judged
a winner. Announcement of all winners is being
made in the November issue of Motor Trend, a
copy of which is enclosed.

Your prize, the bull nose chrome trim, is being
sent to you directly from the supplier and should
reach you shortly.

We wish to thank you for your interest in the
contest and to extend our congratulations on
your being chosen one of the 12 winners from
the many entries.

Sincerely,

MOTOR TREND MAGAZINE

Walter A. Woron
Editor

WAW:cm
enc.

Letter from *Motor Trend* notifying author that he was one of the twelve winners in
its contest.

and now, trucks of about a one-ton capacity and larger have full float-ing rear axles. Also, some four-wheel drive vehicles nowadays use a front hub cap that is different from that on the rear wheels; they are removed by prying off with a screwdriver or a similar tool.

Sometime between April 1917, when this car left the assembly line in Hamtramck (Detroit), and January 1953, when I bought it, it may have been in a minor accident. Apparently it tipped over on its right side or something equally minor. My clues were (1) the right side of the top framework was dented in several places, and (2) the right head-light mounting bracket was attached to the right front fender using a type of screw that was different from those on the left side (and the left side looked to me to be more likely the 1917 type). None of the wooden top bows were broken or cracked, and no other damage was visible to me under my close inspection. This led me to conclude that either whatever happened was repaired properly or the damage was very minor.

After I had finished restoring this car's appearance with new paint and a new top and so on, I happened to see an article in *Motor Trend* that intrigued me. The magazine was having a contest to see what read-ers were doing to their cars with bolt-on accessories. The rules were that cars with cutting and welding were not eligible; only things that were added, or bolted on, would be considered. Since I had a good pic-ture of the right rear three-quarter view of the car, showing most of its accessories, I sent it in as an entry. Much to my astonishment it won a prize! The prize was a bullnose molding. A bullnose molding was used to replace a hood ornament. At that time it was a customizing trend to remove the gaudy hood ornament found on most U.S. cars and to fill in the empty holes left when it was removed. A bullnose mold-ing could be installed instead of filling in the holes. It was a chrome strip, rounded smooth on both ends, that mounted exactly in the holes left where the hood ornament had been and was even the exact con-tour of the hood.

Obviously, there were no bullnose moldings for a forty-year-old 1917 Dodge Brothers touring car, so the magazine sent me a certificate for the retail value of the molding and a catalog from an auto acces-sory company. I selected a set of excellent-quality jumper cables. They cost more than the certificate from the magazine so I sent along my check for the difference. This turned out to be a good investment as I had them for thirty-five years. Once I had to replace the plastic handles, and another time I had to replace the ends themselves. When it came time to replace the ends again, I noticed a lot of green corrosion between the original copper strands, so it was finally time to get a new complete set of cables.

12 · 1946 Hudson

This was a 1946 Hudson three-passenger coupe. It was the Super Six series, which was among the lowest priced. The higher-priced model was the Commodore. My car had several Commodore features, possibly because it was the habit of dealers in 1946 to load up new cars with accessories because customers were so anxious to get new cars then that they would pay exorbitant prices for things such as the big fancy hub caps, a fancy steering wheel with a horn ring, extra bumper guards, and so on.

Since the late 1930s every Hudson, regardless of model, had the hood open from the rear; the hinge was at the front. It was counterbalanced, so when it was raised it was almost perpendicular to the ground and would stay in position. Normal servicing of underhood items was easy, even checking the water in the radiator. The hood was heavy because it was so big. I didn't trust it to stay open so I took a wooden board about 1" × 6" and cut it to fit between the rear brace of the hood and the top of the cowl at the center. I cut a notch in each end of the board so that one end fit inside the hood brace and the other end fit the cowl when the hood was open. I kept this board under the front seat so that it was handy every time I raised the hood.

These Hudsons also had a simple yet strong hood release mounted inside the car alongside the steering column and under the dash board. When the driver pulled into a gas station he would push the handle down to release the hood; when the attendant had finished checking the oil and lowered the hood, the driver pulled the handle back up into the locked position. It was impossible to open the hood from outside the car when locked.

The first of the major postwar updates appeared in 1947 and were

The author's 1946 Hudson three-passenger coupe.

by Studebaker. The giants of the U.S. auto industry, Ford, General Motors and Chrysler Corporation, each made their major changes for their 1949 models.

Because this car was a Hudson it wasn't worth all that many dollars in 1953. I traded in my 1936 Dodge three-passenger coupe and had a car ten years newer not needing the repairs that the 1936 Dodge was going to be needing soon. For about the first six months the car ran very well, and I could not understand why Hudsons were no more valuable than they were, and then I found out! The engine developed a knock like a connecting rod knock. I got two professional opinions and both were the same. It was the center main bearing.

Access to the connecting rods and center main bearing was gained merely by removing a large inspection cover on the bottom of the engine (somewhat like a Model T Ford). I replaced the bearing with a .001 undersize, and it was quiet for a few months. Then I replaced the bottom half only with a .002 undersize and left the .001 in the upper half.

It seems that whoever designed the engine in the 1930s thought that three main bearings were enough for the attainable speeds at the time. Chevrolet had only three main bearings in its early "stove bolt six" engines. As better carburetion, ignition, gasoline, manifolding, and so on were developed, engines ran faster, but no allowance was made for the extra vibration and strain on the crankshaft. Chevrolet and others changed to four main bearings in the mid-1930s, but apparently Hudson could not afford to retool to change its engine.

There were only three other problems I had with this car. One was that the clutch stopped working without warning. Hudson was the only U.S. auto manufacturer to still use a "wet" clutch. This meant that it ran in oil. The facings on the clutch plate were made of cork instead of asbestos. The special oil was to keep the corks supple. The Hudson clutch had two drawbacks: It could fail without warning, and it could not be slipped as that would ruin the corks. You never saw a Hudson with a trailer hitch! Real Hudson enthusiasts would tell you that the Hudson clutch had no equal for smoothness. All modern automatic transmissions have the clutches running in oil. I did not have the facilities to replace the clutch myself so I had it done. Unfortunately it leaked a little after that, which it had not done before. I had to keep adding Hudsonite fluid to the clutch.

The second problem I had with this car was minor, yet persistent. Every two or three months the starter bendix drive would slip when engaging the flywheel. Allowing this to continue would have ruined the ring gear on the flywheel, so I would remove the starter assembly and clean the bendix drive thoroughly with whatever solvent was at hand. The starter was easy to remove but inconvenient in cold weather.

The third problem was that the headlights would sometimes go out without warning. I feel certain that replacing the headlight switch would have corrected the problem, but I never got around to doing so. I also replaced the battery but do not consider this a problem but only a normal maintenance item. I was able to get a rebuilt six-volt battery for $5.00 with a six-month guarantee. It was still working properly when I sold the car about eighteen months later.

When the sheet metal water jacket cover on the left side of the engine block rusted through, I replaced it. Had the incurable flaw of the center main bearing not existed I probably would have kept the car for more than about two years. I sold it while the engine was still quiet and bought #13.

When I bought this car one of the tires was only fair, and the spare didn't look at all reliable. The first November I had the car I decided to buy recap snow tires, trading in the two just described. My snow tires were not the mud/snow type but were ones with smaller grippers. This made them a lot quieter running, and they were adequate for my driving as I never got stuck or had even a close call. Since they were recaps I did not want to remove them from the wheels in the spring. I had no idea how old they were or whether a bead would break during removal or reinstallation. I left them on the car with no bad effects.

This car had no turn signals so I bought an aftermarket kit and added them myself. The two taillights connected without incident, wired in through the brake lights. However, the factory front parking-light fixtures, mounted on tops of the front fenders, were meant strictly as Hudson parking lights only and were not large enough inside to accommodate double-contact light bulbs. My solution was to use the original parking lights as turn signals and disconnect the parking lights.

Like all aftermarket turn signal kits, the switch was to be mounted just under the steering wheel. There was a little rubber wheel inside the switch which, when the switch was positioned correctly on the steering column, would protrude when the switch lever was moved either way and rubbed on the underside of the steering wheel hub. When the driver completed the turn, the rubber would rub a lever on the inside of the switch and move the lever back to the center, turning off the switch. The little rubber wheel would then retract so it no longer contacted the steering wheel hub until the next time the driver moved the switch lever to signal the next intended turn.

Hudson made its major postwar change for its 1948 models. It was called the "step down" design, being quite low to the ground. Hudson retained the 1948 styling through its merger with Nash in 1954, when it became part of American Motors. A few Hudson Ramblers were built to give Hudson dealers the Nash Rambler to sell. The last Hudson was the 1957 model.

As an independent manufacturer, Hudson could not afford to make body changes any more than it could afford to make major engine changes. It had updated its body design for its 1941 models, with the running boards exposed. For its 1942 models Hudson made panels for the door bottoms to cover the running boards. The quarter panels were also given similar panels for the bottoms to match the door panel extensions. Stainless steel moldings were added to the joint seam where the panels were added to conceal the seams. Since the 1942 selling season was so short and the 1946 and 1947 models were almost identical, the extra panels and moldings were also used on the 1946 and 1947 models.

13 · 1940 Dodge

When I learned that the 1946 Hudson (#12) had a major engine design flaw I realized that having the crankshaft machined was the only way to stop the center main bearing from continuing to go bad. That involved removing the engine in order to remove the crankshaft. I did not have the facilities to make those repairs, and I did not think the car was worth the money I would have to pay a mechanic to do the work. My solution was to get a different car.

I began looking for a six-cylinder Chrysler four-door sedan, standard transmission and no fluid drive. In early 1956 I found a dark gray 1940 Dodge; it was the medium-priced model, four-door sedan with the horn ring and big grille guards, like #9, but already in place on the car. It was basically a good solid car but had dented fenders and a bald right rear tire. Since the car cost only $65.00 I could tolerate those things along with the chattering clutch. On the way home from getting the car I stopped at a used tire store and bought a good, high-tread 6.00 × 16 tire for $5.00 installed. The inside of the car was nice and clean and the paint polished up well. Eventually I had the clutch replaced to stop the chatter.

As a routine matter I removed the wheels to inspect the brakes after I had the car for about six months. The linings were thin but the car still stopped properly. I replaced the brake shoes on all four wheels the first chance I had, which was about two weeks later.

For reasons known only to the Chrysler Corporation, all its automobiles and light trucks had a unique type of emergency brake system; it was on the drive shaft, bolted onto the back end of the transmission, whether standard, fluid drive, or automatic. It was operated by a cable and/or levers, depending on exactly which make and

DODGE LUXURY LINER SPECIAL *Four-Door Sedan*

The author's 1940 Dodge Sedan was just like this catalog drawing except that the author's car had the large accessory bumper/grille guards.

model was involved. This was the same basic principle as the Model T Ford foot brake with one big exception: The Model T foot brake was inside the transmission and was meant to bring the moving Ford to a stop. Chrysler, on the other hand, built cars with the brake on the outside of the transmission (on the back of it), and it was meant to *hold* the car *after* the vehicle had already been stopped by the car's regular four-wheel hydraulic brakes. Since Chrysler's emergency brake was not normally applied by the driver while the car was in motion, it never wore out unless a driver forgot to release it and drove with it applied.

If one ever watches a Model T Ford being stopped from a fairly fast speed it will be obvious that the Ford rocks back and forth when it stops. This is due to the action of the ring and pinion gears inside the differential working against the planetary transmission. Every part behind the transmission is part of the braking system, and every part strains a little every time the Ford stops. One can also observe this phenomenon while watching an old 1920s movie where a Model T Ford is used.

Another innovation introduced by Chrysler on all its 1940 models was safety rim wheels. Prior to that time, a tire deflating suddenly, such as a blowout, would likely start to come off the outer rim of the wheel. This could easily cause the drive to lose control of the car, especially if a front tire blew out. Chunks of the tire or inner tube could become wedged or tangled in the steering mechanism or tie rods, jerking the steering wheel out of the driver's hands. A rear tire blowout would cause the back of the car to sway, or "fish tail" so that the driver could not steer the car when the tire and inner tube began to come off the wheel's outer rim. Chrysler's solution to this dilemma was to add an extra flange on the inner portion of the wheel's outer rim. This had the effect of locking both edges of the tire onto the wheel, held further by the air pressure inside the inner tube. If a tire blew out it would deflate immediately and without warning, causing anxious moments for the driver, but at least the tire and inner tube would remain on the wheel.

Chrysler, like all other auto manufacturers, had no control over which brand of tire the customer bought after the original equipment ones wore out. At this time, 1940, most gas stations were equipped to repair an ordinary nail puncture flat tire. The customer had already changed the flat tire and merely brought it in to the gas station. The station attendant pried the bead of the tire off the outer rim of the wheel, carefully working the inner tube out, located the puncture, and then installed a hot patch on the inner tube and a patch on the inside of the tire. Then everything was reassembled and inflated. When the customer returned, everything was ready at a nominal charge. Chrysler's new wheels required a special tool/fixture to remove the tire from the wheel. This apparatus resembled a modern tire-changing machine. It took a while for every tire dealer and gas station to acquire the new tool/machine. It would also work on other wheels as well as pre-1940 Chrysler wheels.

A few years earlier, during the early and mid-1930s, the B.F. Goodrich Tire Company made a tire with a special inner liner that prevented the tire from coming off the wheel. Goodrich's approach was different in that it made an inner liner in the tire itself which was strong enough to keep the sides of the tire rigid enough not to go flat. They were a real bear to get on or off the wheel because the sides were so stiff, but in theory they never had to come off the wheel until the tread wore out.

Chrysler made major styling changes for all 1940 models. Because of the interruption of World War II (when no new cars were produced for over three years), the bodies and chassis were basically unchanged through the early 1949 models. Only fenders, grilles, and minor trim were changed; front doors were given a smooth wave to blend in with the wider fenders on the 1946 through the early 1949 models. Mechanically, the only major change for Dodge was the addition of fluid drive beginning with its 1941 models. The clutch and standard transmission were unchanged; the fluid drive was added between the engine and clutch to achieve a much smoother start.

This 1940 Dodge was the last model Dodge without fluid drive; it ran exceptionally well and was very pleasant to drive. For a couple of years I had been casually looking for a 1949 through 1952 Chrysler six or DeSoto with standard transmission and no fluid drive. One turned up on the used-car lot of Chevrolet dealer in town. When I bought it, this 1940 Dodge became an extra car. A friend thought that it would be an ideal car on which his wife could learn to drive since it had new brakes and a new clutch and the fenders were already dented. He agreed to buy it for a little more than what I had invested in it. He figured that it would be cheaper to do this than to run the risk of his wife's having a mishap with their new-model car. She became a good driver without bumping into anything but would probably have learned more quickly had someone other than her husband been her teacher.

Most of the six-cylinder Chryslers of this era used a pedal to step on to activate the starter. Many General Motors and some independent U.S. auto makers also used a similar arrangement. From constant use the shaft on the plunger on this car had become bent and would not always go down. This meant that I had to reach down and twist the shaft and push it by hand until it worked. I never knew when it was going to act up. The only solution was to replace it, and the only way to do this was to replace the complete assembly, including the spring, pedal, and so on. The parts book I had showed that Plymouth used the same part number. Calls to every Dodge and Plymouth dealer in the area turned up nothing. Finally, a couple of trips to junkyards turned up a good used one. Replacing the assembly was about a fifteen-minute job.

It was not long before I wished I had not sold this car. This is the same regret I had shortly after I sold the 1923 Dodge Brothers touring car (#5). Of the forty cars I have owned, these are the only two I wish I had kept because each one ran so well.

14 · 1951 DeSoto

This was a 1951 DeSoto deluxe club coupe (two door) with the standard transmission and no fluid drive I had been seeking. The 1940 Dodge (#13) ran exceptionally well, but for a while I had been casually looking for a 1949 through 1952 Chrysler six or a DeSoto with standard transmission and no fluid drive. They were very few and far between. Since retail customers for cars in that price range wanted fluid drive with semiautomatic transmission, no dealer would order a standard transmission car except on special order for a customer or as a low-ball price special. This was the lowest-priced car DeSoto made that year, the deluxe club coupe with the standard transmission and no radio, blackwall tires, the cheap two-spoke steering wheel, small hub caps, and so on. The higher-priced model was the Custom. All Custom and most deluxe models had the semiautomatic transmission with fluid drive. Chrysler cars were also available with standard transmission and no fluid drive during those years; they were even rarer than the DeSoto.

I found this car on a used-car lot of a Chevrolet dealer for a price I could handle. It was clean and ran well. It was the newest and nicest car I had at the time. The only real drawbacks were that the doors were huge (as they are on all two-door cars) and that the front seat back was split (as it must be on all two-door cars). I became aware of the importance of seat belts about this time and bought a set of lap belts at an auto supply store. Lap belts were the only type available then. I drilled the floor of this car to install them.

For some reason I never understood, the dashboards of these 1951 through 1954 DeSoto cars had an extension bringing the dash panel all the way down to the floor at about a forty-five-degree angle. It was held in place with screws and clips. It was necessary to remove this to

Top: The author's 1951 DeSoto club coupe after the large hood ornament had been removed and the holes filled in.
   Bottom: The author's 1951 DeSoto as it enters DeSoto County, Florida.

gain access to everything under the dashboard, including the fuse box. To simplify future repairs or maintenance I took the panel off and left it off until I was ready to sell the car.

This car, as did many cars of the era, had a monstrous hood ornament. This DeSoto had a profile of a Spanish military man of the Middle Ages wearing a metal helmet and armor. Hernando DeSoto was a Spanish explorer in the Americas in the sixteenth century. To prevent the hood ornament from injuring anyone who might bump into it, I removed it, filled in the holes properly, sanded everything smooth and refinished the area. About ten days after this, a lad of about ten ran into the front of the car on his bicycle while the car was stopped. He landed on the hood but was not injured; no one even wants to think about what might have happened had that hood ornament still been there. The picture shows the car after I had removed the ornament and filled in the holes.

The 1949 and 1950 DeSoto grilles were different, but each had vertical grille bars. This 1951 DeSoto was the first of several models with the grilles having individual "teeth"; each tooth was different. Perhaps they were meant to be a copy of the 1950 Buick front bumper teeth.

When I bought this car I bought an accessory for it that I wound up buying for most of the cars I had from then on: a locking gas cap. For a short time I carried the key to it on my key ring with the rest of my keys, but that was a bit of a bother, and it made one more key to carry around. Then I hit upon the idea of getting a key chain about eight inches long, just long enough to hold one key and to fit over the emergency brake handle. By that time emergency brake controls were on the left side, under the dashboard between the steering column and the driver's door. When the control evolved to the step-on style, a release handle was located in the same area. When I would drive into a gas station I would merely remove it and then return it when I was ready to leave. I never lost a key and I always knew where it was.

When I found this car it did not have a radio or a clock. I located a new clock at the DeSoto dealer across town, but the parts manager insisted on full retail price for it. My efforts to explain to him that the clock was now obsolete and that his chances of selling it at full retail were nonexistent fell on deaf ears. He would not budge on the price, and I presume he still had it when the dealership went out of business a few years later. I found a good radio and clock in a junkyard and installed them myself. The push button radio for the 1951 through 1954 DeSotos had the tuning knob and the volume control together on the same side of the radio; the outside knob controlled one and the inside knob controlled the other. The only sound system available was AM; hi-fi FM stereo and tape players were unavailable at the time in automobile radios.

When this car was new, DeSoto sponsored Groucho Marx on radio and later on, television as well as radio; Buick sponsored Milton Berle and then later Jackie Gleason; Chevrolet sponsored Dinah Shore; Dodge sponsored Lawrence Welk; and Lincoln Mercury sponsored Ed Sullivan. Groucho was personally involved with the guests on his programs, often ordinary people. This made his zany personality come across to the audience more than the other auto sponsors' celebrities. Groucho died at the age of eighty-six on August 19, 1977 (three days after Elvis Presley died).

In the summer of 1956 I made a two-week vacation trip of 2,500 miles to Ft. Lauderdale in this car. The interstate system was still mostly on the drawing board at the time, but I was traveling on an excellent four-lane divided highway in Georgia when I was pulled over for speeding by a state trooper. He said I had been going 80 but had slowed down when around other traffic. I knew better than to argue with a police officer. I readily produced my driver's license, registration and proof of insurance. He could see that everything was in order and since I was not driving dangerously, he just gave me a warning. I had not realized that I was speeding, and I heeded the posted limit for the rest of the trip.

I kept this car for about eighteen months, selling it only after I found a four-door sedan with standard transmission that I liked better because it was a four door, #16.

When I decided to sell this car I advertised it in the Sunday newspaper and a fellow came to see it. He wasn't overly enthusiastic about the car, so I was wondering why he had come to see it in the first place. Then he made a very strange request of me; he asked to see the title. Then he compared the serial number on the title with the one on the car's left front hinge post; they were different. One of the seven numbers had been typed wrong. Apparently that gave him the excuse he was looking for as he used that as his reason for not buying it. I assured him that I would have the title corrected, but he still refused to consider it.

A couple of days later I drove the car to the court house where the title had been issued. I copied down the correct number from the car and took it and the title into the auto title department. The clerk there researched the previous title (where the previous owner had traded the car in to the Chevrolet dealer) and found where the mistake had been made. I was issued a new, corrected title at no cost to me. Had I bothered to check the number myself I would have had the mistake corrected on my own. I now check serial numbers with paperwork as soon as I get them. I wonder what excuse that fellow would use not to buy the car now.

15 • 1930 Ford

A friend of mine had restored all the mechanical parts on a 1930 Ford Fordor (four-door) Town Sedan, with the blank quarter panels instead of quarter windows and fold-down arm rest in the rear seat back. He had also painted the body maroon with black fenders and aprons. He told me that while he was sanding down the paint on the doors he had come across the original paint and markings of a Yellow Cab. He enjoyed the car a lot for a short time but then found a 1931 Model A Ford rumble-seat roadster, a much more desirable and valuable car than the four-door sedan.

The roadster was in excellent mechanical condition. My friend had done a body-off restoration of the roadster, switching the mechanical components from the sedan to the roadster since he knew they were perfect (he had just rebuilt them all), using new gears, bearings, and other parts during the rebuilding. I helped him switch over the front axle assembly as well as the engine, transmission and rear axle assemblies out of both cars. The roadster wound up with the freshly restored parts, and the sedan got all the very good parts. It was mainly a matter of removing nuts and bolts, raising things up and removing and installing complete assemblies.

Along the way my friend found some extra Model A Ford parts.

Opposite Top: The author's 1930 Model A Ford. The body is somewhat unusual in that it had blank rear quarter panels (that is, no quarter windows). When the original paint was sanded down, markings beneath showed that it had originally been a taxi cab. The rear seat had an arm rest in the center which could be up or down as rear passengers desired; that was also a somewhat unusual feature on a low-priced car such as a Ford.

Opposite Bottom: Rear view of the author's 1930 Ford showing the Florida license plate, the two taillights, and the spare tire cover.

The only item he had not tackled on the sedan was the upholstery. The car drove nicely and was very presentable from the outside.

After getting a good start on the roadster restoration, my friend decided to sell the sedan. I bought it from him, and it turned out to have one major incurable mechanical problem. The gasoline mileage was four miles per gallon! Everyone told me that was impossible. I checked for gasoline leaks; there weren't any. The car ran beautifully. I checked for dragging brakes; they weren't. I even found a new, still-in-the-box carburetor — no help. On several occasions I filled the gas tank, drove about 35 miles or so and had to add almost ten gallons to fill the ten-gallon tank again. I did not depend just on the odometer but on distances I had known for a long time. All the adjustments on the engine were checked several times by me and others; they were always correct. For a while I ran the carburetor so lean that it burned an intake valve. Replacing it made the engine run properly again but did not improve the gas mileage at all.

Another problem was annoying but easily fixed. I could not depend on both headlights to come on at the same time. Sometimes one would come on, and sometimes neither, and once in a while both would come on together. The problem turned out to be the connector at each headlight. Fixing the problem merely required removing the original connectors where the wire fittings were butted against one another and replacing them with modern push-in blade-type connectors.

Had the gas mileage problem not existed I would have finished restoring the car by having the bumpers rechromed, getting the upholstery redone, getting the wheels painted, and buying new hub caps, plus a few other minor items.

There was only one original taillight on the left rear fender when I bought it, just like every Model A when it left the Ford assembly plant. Original lights with the original lens and the brackets were still available, and I found a complete set of everything. It was a reasonably simple matter to drill the right rear fender in exactly the right places and to add the necessary wiring.

The friend from whom I had bought this car had several excellent 4.50 × 19 tires, five of which came with this car plus one or two more that were slightly worn. He had planned to get new tires for the 1931 roadster he was restoring. One afternoon, while I was driving about three or four miles from home, the left rear tire blew out. It happened on a flat street that was two lanes in each direction, and the car fishtailed over both of my lanes before I was able to get it stopped. I had been going about 25 miles an hour, I suppose, and I was thankful that no other cars were around at the time. The incident took me by complete surprise, which is why the car fishtailed before I could get it under control. After regaining my composure it was a simple matter to change the tire and put the spare on, then later replace the blown-out tire and tube on the wheel with one of the slightly worn ones as the spare.

When I left on a vacation trip to Ft. Lauderdale in #14, the 1951 DeSoto, I brought along the title to this 1930 Ford. I thought it would raise a few eyebrows if a twenty-six-year-old car had a license plate from a resort area so far away. I easily and legally obtained a Florida license plate and title. The following year I got my new license plate by mail, also easily and legally.

I really enjoyed driving that Model A but just could not afford to keep gasoline in it. My modern DeSoto, a much heavier car with a six-cylinder engine, gave much better gas mileage. After about a year I sold the Ford to a fellow who lived about 300 miles away.

When sales of the Model T Ford dropped in the mid-1920s Ford attempted to revive the car by giving every one a starter in 1925, then by reducing tire and wheel size from 23 inches (30 × 31/2) to 21 inches and also lowering the axle spindles to make the car lower. Nothing was done to improve the major flaws of the basic Model T design, however. Finally, in the spring of 1927, shortly after Model T number 15,000,000 was built, Model T production ceased.

A new model was introduced in late 1927 as a 1928 model, the Model A. Unfortunately, the major chassis design was retained, although updated somewhat. The two-speed planetary transmission was replaced with one with a gearshift lever (stick) in the middle of the floor, having three speeds and a clutch, like all other U.S.-built cars. The foot brake inside the transmission was replaced with mechanical brakes on all four wheels operated by levers and rods. The steering gear was no longer directly under the steering wheel at the top of the steering column but was now bolted to the frame, under the hood, the way other U.S. car manufacturers had been doing for many, many years. The cooling system now had a water pump to cut down on overheating.

Except for the addition of a shock absorber at each wheel, the basic chassis suspension design remained exactly the same with only one spring per axle and braces, nicknamed "wishbones," to keep each axle from twisting. Wire wheels with 21-inch tires were retained.

Bodies were made lower, and the paint finish as well as upholstery fabrics were now available in more colors. The magneto ignition was replaced by a distributor type. The engine was the same basic design but was improved to go faster and was given an oil pump and an oil dip stick. The generator was now driven by a belt instead of gears; the same belt also drove the water pump.

The 1928 and 1929 Model A were almost identical, then changes were made for the 1930 Model A. The chassis and running gear were, for the most part, unchanged. Wheel and tire size was reduced from 21 inches to 19 inches, mainly for looks, although this lowered the car by one inch. The rest of the major changes were appearance changes. The bodies were made lower and more rounded, and a few more body styles were added, also more paint and upholstery colors. Fenders and aprons were also given a more modern, pleasant appearance. The radiator shell (covering) was now stainless steel, which Ford referred to as "rustless steel." The 1931 Model A, the last Model A, contained almost no changes, except for the addition of a few more body styles and the radiator shell on all 1931s having a raised panel in the upper part which was painted the same color as the body.

This was the oldest of any of the cars I had to come from the factory with any safety glass, and that was for the windshield only. My 1917 Dodge Brothers, 1921 Ford, 1923 Dodge Brothers and 1923 Lincoln were all open cars, the only glass being the two-piece windshield in each. Until the mid-1930s safety glass was standard equipment in the windshield only, with side and rear windows being regular glass. Side and rear windows of safety glass were available as a factory installed accessory package during the early and mid-1930s only. Eventually so many customers were ordering the safety glass side and rear window accessory package that all manufacturers made it standard equipment.

Although it was possible for a dealer to remove standard glass and replace it with safety glass, it was not financially practical. The dealer would have had to buy the safety glass package, then pay the mechanic to change them over, a job requiring several hours to complete. The dealer would then have the removed panes of regular glass in his parts inventory, which he could probably never sell. At the assembly plant, however, all anyone had to do was to pick up the safety glass from one stack instead of the regular glass from the other stack; labor costs were the same.

This 1930 Ford, like all 1928 through 1931 Model A's, had the gas tank mounted on top of the cowl with the filler cap in the center of the cowl, just in front of the windshield. The cowl-mounted gas tank was a carryover from the Model T's last year of production. One exception was that there was a gauge on the dashboard of the Model A. Since the tank was immediately in front of the dashboard a float-type gauge was used. It would cause an indicator to move on the dashboard; there were no electrical connections or wiring. Because each different gasoline refiner put different dyes into its gasoline, the gasoline in the gauge was the same color as the most recent gasoline purchase.

It wasn't until Ford's 1932 models that the gas tank on all Ford automobiles was mounted at the rear of the chassis and a mechanical fuel pump ran off the engine's camshaft to pump the fuel into the carburetor of both the four- and eight-cylinder models.

This was the newest car I owned that came factory equipped with a drum-type speedometer. Instead of a dial with a pointer that we are used to nowadays the speedometer showed only the actual speed of the car. Most makes of cars were equipped with this type of unit from about 1915 through the 1920s. The most popular brand was made by Stewart-Warner. The only real drawback was that the speedometer would not register above 60 mph. By the end of the 1920s roads and cars had been so much improved that 60 mph was attainable with most medium- and high-priced cars. The dial-type speedometer could be calibrated up to 100 or even 120 mph even though it was neither possible nor safe to drive that fast at that time. Speedometers of the era were driven by a flexible cable running between the transmission and the dashboard.

16 · *1950 DeSoto*

In the spring of 1957, without looking too hard I found a 1950 DeSoto four-door sedan with a standard transmission. DeSoto made its standard transmission cars only as deluxe models, which, contrary to the normal meaning of the word were the cheapest model. The fancy, expensive model was the "Custom." I was able to buy this car because the price was low. The price was low for two reasons: First, it was the cheapest model with the standard transmission, and second, it had been hit on the right side. The front door was beyond hope, but the rear door and rear fender were dented only slightly. I knew I could fix them myself.

A few Saturdays later a friend of mine, who was something of an automotive enthusiast and tinkerer, went to a junkyard about 20 miles out in the country with me. I hit the jackpot. I found a 1951 DeSoto Suburban, which was similar to the Frazer Vagabond of that era in that the door upholstery was a leather like material, including the arm rests.

The Suburban/Vagabond body was split across the back so the back window and sheet metal around it could be raised and the trunk could be lowered like a tailgate. The right front door of this car was perfect; it was even the same color as my car. The junkyard car was the Custom model with the fancier steering wheel, wheel covers, and several other goodies.

When my friend and I carried all the parts I had removed into the junkyard office, the owner respected all the work I had done to remove them and gave me a very friendly price for everything.

Replacing the door was a fairly quick and easy job as was changing over the lock cylinders so that the original key still worked the door lock. Replacing the steering wheel, inside door trims, and other goodies took another weekend or two. Several months later, I replaced the tires with wide whitewall Firestones. I also painted the rim of each wheel black enamel; so often these are left alone and rusty and don't look nice. The wide whitewalls on the black rims and stainless steel wheel covers on the dark green car made it look distinguished, especially since I kept the car polished and shiny.

The 1950 DeSoto had a hood ornament just as big as the 1951's. Although they would not interchange because the slope of the hoods was slightly different between the 1950 and 1951 models, both ornaments were equally hazardous to anyone who might bump into them. To avoid any possibility of problems I removed this one and filled in the

Top: The author's 1950 DeSoto showing the leather like door and arm rest trim removed from a DeSoto Suburban. It was very easy to keep clean and never showed any wear.

Bottom: The author's 1950 DeSoto after the gaudy hood ornament had been removed. It was metallic dark green.

1951 FRAZER

The Pride of Willow Run   page 141

*The famous successor to the station wagon
...the 2-cars-in-1 Frazer Vagabond
converts in 10 seconds from luxurious
6-passenger sedan to spacious carrier.*

Top: DeSoto also made a vehicle with the back end opening up like this 1951 Frazer.
On a DeSoto like this the author found the door upholstery trim panels.

Bottom: Rear view of the author's 1950 DeSoto with slightly modified 1952 taillights. This car never had backup lights.

An ad for a 1950 DeSoto showing the gaudy hood ornament which the author removed from his 1950 DeSoto.

holes just as I had done on the 1951 DeSoto, #14. Thankfully, no incidents occurred. The picture shows the car after the ornament was removed and the holes filled and the area repainted. I fixed the right rear door and fender shortly after I bought the car.

This car gave only one real problem during the five years I owned it. One Sunday at home I heard a noise coming from the right front wheel. I removed the right front wheel cover and grease cap to find that the wheel bearing had started to come apart. I knew I couldn't drive it very far. There was a gas station that also did repairs about half a block away so I drove it very slowly. I knew that the mechanic would not be there on Sunday so I left the car there. Monday evening I returned to find it all ready. What I had not realized was that the mechanic had burned the bearing roller cage and inner race off with a cutting torch to get the parts off the spindle.

The problem didn't show up again until another Sunday afternoon about four years later. This time I was driving on the interstate in the city. There were no other cars around. Without any warning the car was impossible to steer; it took up all three lanes of the roadway. I slowed down and was able to pull completely off the right side of the road onto the shoulder.

I decided to jack up the right front wheel to investigate the problem. The only help I had with me were tools to change a tire. I set my tripod bumper jack properly, and as soon as the weight came off the wheel, the wheel, brake drum and half of the spindle fell off. The other half of the spindle remained attached to the suspension. It was obvious that I wasn't going to move that car without a tow truck. My only explanation for being able to get that car stopped safely and completely off the road is that this was just one more example of how God takes care of me!

I had no choice but to put the wheel, with the parts still attached to it, on the rear floor of the car. I also put the ignition key there and left a door unlocked. I don't like to leave a car that way, but I had no choice because the two truck driver would need them the next morning.

The first thing Monday morning I called a friend who operated a small garage with his father. He had the car towed in and bought a used suspension from a junkyard and replaced the broken one. By this time I had owned this car for about five years, but this incident made me lose all confidence in it. Two weeks later I had a different car. Until the broken spindle incident that car was very dependable.

One of several vacation trips I made in that car was up through New England one October. The leaves were changing color, and it is hard to describe how beautiful the autumn scenery is unless it is actually seen. I had a list of every old car museum in several states and visited just about every one. While in Boston I asked a policeman how to get to Larz Anderson Park. He said, "You want to go to Lahz An'son Pahk?" It seems that Larz Anderson was an extremely wealthy man who, from the late nineteenth century until about 1930, bought some very unusual cars, all very expensive. He never sold a car or traded one in on another one. He is supposed to have kept every car he ever bought.

There was a huge carriage house behind the Anderson mansion, where the cars were kept. By the time I was there the Anderson family had donated the property to the state, I believe, with the provision that it keep the estate intact and, of course, let people see it. I don't recall how many acres the entire estate contained, but it was big enough to turn into a park. Various old car clubs in the area have occasionally received permission to hold shows there.

I had planned that trip to coincide with the old car show at Hershey, Pennsylvania. Even then it was a gigantic affair. I spent all day Saturday there and I think managed to make only one complete trip through the flea market. I saw the acres and acres of old cars but just did not have time to do more than glance at them while going to and from the flea market.

Hershey is near Harrisburg, the capital of Pennsylvania, and in the center of the state. To get there from New England means traveling on the Pennsylvania Turnpike, now part of the interstate system, but not at that time. Originally designed as a route for a railroad, the railroad project ran out of money. Tunnels were made through many of the Allegheny mountains. Eventually the state took it over and converted it to a limited-access highway for automobiles, trucks, and buses. In autumn the mountains' millions of trees and leaves all seem to be a different fall color. In several places you cannot see the entrance to a tunnel until you are within about a mile of it. All you see in front of you is leaves, so you get the impression that you are driving into a wall of autumn colors.

Going west, the Ohio Turnpike meets the Pennsylvania Turnpike. By then the mountains are behind you. At dusk I looked through the windshield and saw the sun just at the horizon and then looked in the rear-view mirror and saw stars in the dark sky. The New England vacation was only one of several vacations I made in this car. I also made numerous weekend trips to various car shows closer to home. I enjoyed driving it and the delightful way it rode.

Once when I had a day off from work I was driving and came to a traffic light. I stepped down on the accelerator as I wanted to try to make it through. At that instant the top radiator hose split and sprayed water (or whatever was in the radiator at the time) all over the top of the flathead, six-cylinder engine, shorting out the electrical system for a split second. This caused a backfire which blew out the muffler.

There was a Midas Muffler shop about a block away. Those were the days when Midas sold only mufflers and pipes. I made it to Midas very noisily and drove quietly away about $20.00 later. I wrapped several layers of tape around the split hose and bought a new one at an auto parts store on the way home. When things cooled down a little while later I replaced the hose.

I have no idea how long that muffler had been on the car; perhaps it was already thin and ready to go bad anyway. The floor on this car (and on many cars of that era) was flat, with only a slight hump in the rear floor. This allowed air to flow between the floor, the muffler, and pipes. As designers made cars lower to the ground, the floor was no longer flat but was made with wells for people's feet. This prevents air from circulating around the muffler, making it run hotter and go bad sooner.

During the time I owned this car it became an orphan. Chrysler ceased production of DeSoto in late 1960 after building a few 1961 models. I had the car from early 1957 until mid-1962.

When this car was new, backup lights were accessories. They could be added by drilling the correct size hole in the rear lower body panel between the trunk and the rear fender, using the template that came with each light assembly. The car was already wired for two backup lights that would come on when the transmission was shifted into reverse with the ignition switch on. If a customer wanted only one, it would be installed on the left side, but that gave the rear of the car a lopsided look.

This car had neither, and I did not care to add them. For the 1951 models the same backup light fixture came as standard equipment on the left side only, with one for the right side being an accessory. Most of the expensive "Custom" models had them factory installed on both sides.

The taillights themselves were oval fixtures in one housing, with one red lens with a chrome bar horizontally across each chrome bezel about one third of the way down from the top and another about one third of the way up from the bottom. One double-contact bulb illuminated all three sections.

For the 1952 models the separate backup light fixtures were eliminated and were integrated into the taillight fixtures. They fit the 1950 and 1951 fenders exactly. The top two thirds contained the single double-contact bulb with no chrome bar across. There was a chrome bar one third up from the bottom, and the bottom third had the backup lens and a single-contact bulb. Personally, I liked that arrangement better.

On a trip to a junkyard I found two 1952 taillight assemblies. I cut a piece of thick red plastic to the same size as the backup lenses and replaced the original backup lenses with them. Then I rearranged the wiring so that the regular taillights were the single-contact bulbs in the former backup sections and the brake and turn signals were now the big regular ones.

It had been my habit to go over the cylinder head bolts with a torque wrench about every six months to make sure they were tight at 65 pounds pressure. I had been doing this on all my six-cylinder Chrysler cars for a long time. This time one of the bolts broke off. It was one of those near the center of the head and easy to get to without removing anything else.

I went on and finished checking the rest of them. When I started the engine it still ran properly. I knew that eventually the head gasket would blow because the broken bolt would not allow proper pressure on the head and its gasket. Rather than attempt to replace it myself and run the risk of ruining the threads in the cylinder block, I took it to the DeSoto dealer not too far from where I worked at the time, while the car was still running properly.

Their mechanic was able to remove the broken part of the bolt without removing the cylinder head. He had a tool known as an "E-Z out." He drilled a very small hole in the broken end of the bolt and then inserted the E-Z out tool, which has left hand threads. The broken end of the bolt backed right out, and the mechanic installed a new one without problems and without having to remove the cylinder head. I was charged only for the time he actually spent on the repair plus the new bolt. That was the only time I have ever broken off a head bolt by checking them periodically for proper torque.

While driving one summer afternoon with several friends in the car, the person in the right front seat said that a lot of heat was coming from the heater. I checked the controls and all were "off." The first opportunity I had to pull over and stop I raised the hood and found that the plenum chamber door was stuck in the "on" position, allowing the heat to come inside the car. I think I had a pair of vise grips or pliers or something with me and was able to disconnect the operating cable and manually close the plenum chamber door. A few days later I took it apart and put some white grease on the cable and door operating parts to get everything working properly again.

On this car, as on all Chrysler products of 1949 and 1950, the ignition/starter switch was on the far left lower edge of the dashboard, to the left of the steering column, and had to be worked with the left hand. It also had a cigarette lighter on the dashboard, just to the right of the steering column, about half way up the dashboard. Since I had no use for the lighter I removed it and disconnected its wiring, then moved the ignition/starter switch there. It fit perfectly in the hole left by the lighter socket.

A couple of weeks later I removed one of the inside garnish moldings and took it to an auto paint supply store. They looked up the color and mixed me some paint that matched exactly. A friend who had spray painting equipment said he would paint them for me. I sanded everything down very smoothly, masked everything on the dashboard and steering column, and removed the steering wheel so that he could get around everything with his spray gun. The result was beautiful. With the faultless leather like upholstery on the doors and this new paint, the inside of the car was like new.

17 · 1933 Franklin

After disposing of #15, the four-mile-per-gallon Model A Ford, I began looking for another enclosed car. In 1958, the Ike and Mamie days of wholesome family values were soon to give way to the hippie, drug and vandalism days of the 1960s and "anything goes."

In early 1958 I located a 1933 Franklin Olympic coupe. Franklin went bankrupt in 1934, and the Olympic models of 1933 and 1934, in the $1,500 price range, were a desperate attempt to stay in business. A four-door sedan, a rumble seat coupe and a convertible with a rumble seat made up the Olympic line. Other Franklins were classics, but none of the Olympics were.

Except for the engine, the Olympics were almost "assembled" cars. Bodies came from Reo; brake shoes and drums were 1933 Chevrolet, although Franklin had used hydraulic brakes since 1928. All the lights were Guide (also from GM) the taillight being from a 1930 Buick design; the electrical system, other than the lights, consisted of Delco components (also GM). Although I can't say for certain, I am under the impression that the axles, steering, clutch, transmission, and so on were bought from other suppliers for the Olympic and not made by Franklin.

With a 1933 Chevrolet selling for about $500 comparably equipped, it is no wonder that Franklin went bankrupt when trying to get three times as much for its cars. The 1933 Franklin Olympic was not three times better than a 1933 Chevrolet. I have long believed that if Franklin had converted to liquid (water) cooling with a radiator in the mid-1920s, the company could have survived. Franklin spent time making its cars go faster and setting speed and endurance records, but that only made the engines run hotter because the air cooling could not dissi-

Top: The author's 1933 Franklin after painting and chrome, except for grille work, had been completed. The original headlights were restored and reinstalled; the horns could not be repaired and new ones could not be found.

    Bottom: The author's 1933 Franklin "right out of the barn" as it was ready for the 100-mile trip to the author's home.

Top: The author's 1933 Franklin "right out of the barn" in the background. The original horns were mashed as they protruded beyond the bumper and were the first point of contact when a driver pulled into the garage. Also shown are the farm tractor-type headlights.

Bottom: The author's 1933 Franklin after chrome and painting had been completed.

The author's 1933 Franklin after the painting and chrome had been completed, shown with rumble seat closed and open.

pate the heat fast enough. This made the engines overheat, and they were very expensive to rebuild as, once an air-cooled engine overheats, the cylinders and pistons must be replaced. The same situation took place in the late 1960s and early 1970s with the Chevrolet Corvair and the Volkswagen Beetle. They could be made to run very fast but not for very long.

The man from whom I purchased this particular car had seen it being driven back and forth to work every day by a welder. Although not dented, it was not a creampuff by any stretch of the imagination. To the fellow driving it back and forth to work it was just cheap, dependable transportation. It had a blown head gasket, but, since the engine was air cooled, this just meant that one cylinder didn't work and no further damage would result.

The fellow I bought it from convinced the welder to sell it and drive something more modern to and from work. The fellow I knew found a head gasket but had no intention of replacing it as he had two or three other old cars he was restoring. He just bought it to keep it in circulation so it would not be junked by the welder if it ever broke down.

I attempted to replace the head gasket but was unable to get the head separated from the cylinder and took it to an auto machine shop with the head gasket for them to replace. All they could do was to separate the head from the cylinder. They could not get the head back on. I reinstalled the cylinder on the engine and then installed the new gasket and head.

Whatever was wrong to blow the first gasket was still wrong as this gasket also blew immediately. I decided to let the engine go (since it still ran okay except for the noise) and to concentrate on the appearance of the car.

I knew another old car nut who was in the monument business and had sandblasting equipment. After removing the tire, inner tube and flap, I took one of the 17-inch wire wheels to him. When I picked it up a week later and brought him the next wheel, I told him that I would be bringing the others one at a time.

I took the freshly sandblasted wheel and primed it with red oxide primer by hand with a small brush. Then I sanded and brushed on two coats of the correct shade of green enamel. Then I reinstalled the inner tube, flap, and tire. I did this with each wheel, one at a time. The wheels were done in the winter when it was too cold to work on the car itself in the unheated garage, but I could bring one wheel at a time inside the house. All I had to do in the garage was to change one wheel at a time. The entire restoration of all five wheels took six to eight weeks.

Like in most cars of this era, the battery was located under the driver's seat, suspended from the car frame in a tray. This battery box was pretty well rusted away. I removed it and took it to a sheet metal man. He said he could make me a new one provided I was not in a hurry; I wasn't. This was the same winter I was redoing the wheels. I had removed the battery and set it on the concrete garage floor. By the time the new box was ready (about six weeks later) a couple of real cold snaps had been there and gone and the battery had split. The new battery fit the new box perfectly.

This car had a metal tube running above the engine, the full length of the engine, inside of which were spark plug wires. The rear of the tube was bolted to the dashboard and also contained the hot wire from the ignition switch to the distributor near the front of the engine. This wire insulation was dry and cracked, and it was apparent to me that when the bare part of the wire would touch the metal tube, a short circuit would occur, and the engine would stop running and might also short out other electrical components.

To prevent this, I replaced the wire. I disconnected the wire at the front of the engine and then taped a new piece of wire of the same gauge to it and pulled it through the metal tube from under the dash. Then I cut the new wire to the proper length, installed the correct fitting on each end of the wire, and connected each to where it belonged. When I went to start the engine to be sure it was done right, the engine would not start! When I reinstalled the coil wire I had accidentally knocked loose, the engine started. That old wire had been there for twenty-five years.

Another friend who had a compressor, good spray guns, and all the other necessary equipment, including a pickup truck in which to transport everything, agreed to spray the car for me. I removed all the fenders and aprons to be painted black lacquer. I also removed the hood and rumble seat lid to be painted the same green as the body and wheels. I took the hood apart by removing the hinge stiff wire holding each section to the one next to it. I also removed the louver doors on each side hood panel to make those parts come out perfect. Everything was sprayed in lacquer except the enamel I had already put on the wheels. The only parts not removed to be painted were the doors. Since they were aligned properly and could easily be opened wide enough to paint inside, I saw no reason to remove them. I had to raise the body up off the frame to get the side aprons out, but this was by no means a body-off restoration.

I did all the sanding by hand. When I got down to the original 1933 primer I switched from 80D sandpaper to 220 wet, then to 400 wet. The car had been repainted once before during its twenty-five-year life. All the spraying was done over 400 wet sanded surfaces only. My friend would come over every Sunday after church and spray everything I had ready. Then I would spend every evening the following week 400 wet sanding. The paint work turned out beautifully.

Before I reinstalled the rumble seat lid I put new light tan side kick panels in the rumble seat compartment, also a new rubber mat. I also cleaned the original leather cushions to bring them back to their original beauty. I put new light tan kick panels in the front passenger compartment as well as a new rubber floor mat. While everything was apart I had the bumpers, dash fittings, gearshift and emergency brake handles and parts, windshield molding, hood louver handles, center hood hinge, and so on chrome plated. The only things I did not have done were the grille shell and the vertical shutters. That would have been a tremendous expense. Moreover, every rivet in the shutter mechanisms would have had to be drilled out to remove the individual shutters, then replaced and readjusted. That would have been very tedious and time consuming, in addition to costly.

When I bought the car the original stainless steel headlights had been replaced by universal sealed beam assemblies like those someone would buy for a farm tractor. The originals came with the car and were complete and in perfect working order, so I reinstalled them. The original chrome horns were on the car when I bought it but were badly dented in front, and the trumpets were mashed back. They were mashed because their ends stuck out in front beyond the front bumper, so the first time the original owner pulled all the way into the garage, the horn trumpets hit the wall before the bumper. They were too bad to repair and I was never able to locate any good used ones as long as I had the car. Those on the 1933 Doge looked identical, but I was never able to find a good pair of those either. I considered mounting a shell-type horn under the hood, but, believe it or not, there wasn't enough room! The six-cylinder, air-cooled engine took up every bit of available space under the hood.

Had I had the money to get the head gasket replaced or the engine repaired by a Franklin expert I would have done so. Being unable to do so I reluctantly realized that I had to sell the car. A fellow who had restored several Franklins through the years and had the necessary parts to rebuild the engine bought it and got the engine running properly in fairly short order. I saw him with the car a couple of years later, and it still looked as nice as when he bought it from me, thanks to my friend's paint work. He had not had the grille shell and shutters rechromed.

Standard equipment on this car was a Guide taillight made by General Motors and mounted on the left rear fender. The lenses and rim were the same as on the 1930 Buick. I located another lens and rim assembly but neither the body of the light nor the bracket to mount it on the fender. Later I was glad I hadn't located one as I would have been tempted to install it on the right side to give the rear of the car a balanced look. Then I realized that the rumble seat steps were on the right side, and sooner or later someone would use that taillight as a step. The lower step was just above the right end of the bumper, and the second step, both cast aluminum, was on the top of the right rear fender. A taillight would have been about halfway between the steps.

This is the oldest car I owned that had convex headlight lenses. Prior to this the 1917 Dodge Brothers, the 1921 Ford, the 1923 Lincoln, the 1923 Dodge Brothers, the 1925 Dodge Brothers, the 1929 Chevrolet and the 1930 Ford all had flat lenses. Most were removed by using both hands and pushing against the headlight outer rim while twisting it slightly to the left. The flat lens was held to the inside of the rim by little spring clips. With the rim and lens removed you could replace the bulb and clean the inside of the lens and the reflector. The convex types all had the outer rim held on by a screw at the bottom, then by raising the rim and lens straight up slightly, one could disengage it from the headlight body. Bulb replacement was the same until the advent of sealed beams for the 1940 models.

This was the newest car I owned to be equipped with only one taillight as standard equipment. My 1917 Dodge Brothers, 1921 Ford and 1923 Dodge Brothers had only one taillight with one single-contact bulb that went on with the headlights and no brake light. My 1923 Lincoln, 1925 Dodge Brothers, 1929 Chevrolet, 1930 Ford and this 1933 Franklin were factory equipped with one brake light in the same fixture as the one taillight. Each had one single-contact bulb. I added a second taillight to the 1917 Dodge Brothers, but no brake lights. I also added a complete second taillight/brake light fixture on the right side to my 1930 Ford.

Low-priced cars were factory equipped with only one tail/brake light assembly during the 1930s, and this was always mounted on the left side for safety. The second assembly for the right side was available as an accessory. When my father bought the family 1935 Chevrolet and also the family 1936 Chevrolet, he had the dealer add the second brake/taillight accessory package to the right side. The last U.S. auto manufacturer to equip its lowest-priced car with only one tail/brake light was Ford for its standard model in 1941.

Minor style changes took place in the early 1930s on the inside of U.S.-built cars. One was replacing four-spoke steering wheels with the thick rims with the three-spoke type with the thin rim, which was much easier for women to grip. Another rather subtle change was the addition of rubber pads on the clutch and brake pedals. Prior to that time the driver's shoe sole stepped on a steel pedal. If the right shoe happened to be wet, it could slip off the brake pedal onto the gas pedal — with unpleasant results. When the rubber pad became worn on one side it could be turned around to have the driver step on the unworn portion or replaced by loosening one bolt on the back of the pedal. Every car I owned newer than the 1933 had rubber pads on the clutch and brake pedals as standard equipment. Accessory pedal pads were available for a few makes of cars during the 1920s but were not very popular as they wore out quickly.

Another change was the switch to indirect lighting for the dashboard gauges. One fixture with a separate switch protruded from the dashboard to light all (three) dash gauges. The change was to have a small bulb inside each gauge with the gauge recessed slightly in the dashboard. Each light went on when the main light switch was turned on. Expensive cars were given a dimmer device on the dash light circuit.

This was the oldest car I had with snap-on hub caps; they actually covered the lug bolts which held the wheel onto the brake drum on the car. My 1917 Dodge Brothers, 1921 Ford, 1923 Dodge Brothers, 1923 Lincoln and 1929 Chevrolet all had screw-on hub caps. A tool came with each new car specially made to fit the hex fitting on the particular make and model car involved. The screw-on hub cap kept the grease for the particular front wheel bearing from leaking out. In the rear they kept the rear axle parts clean. The bolts actually holding the wheel onto the car were in about an eight-inch circle. Wooden wheels had demountable rims, so they were not removed to change a tire. Cars with wire or disc wheels had the lug bolts exposed and were located outside the hub cap. Wire or disc wheels were removed without disturbing the screw-on hub cap.

My 1930 Ford was equipped with small hub caps with tabs on the outer flanges. With the wheel off the car, the hub cap was held up to the center of the wheel with the tabs inside the opening. The tabs were bent over on the inside to hold the hub cap on. There was no mechanical reason to ever remove the hub cap; it was for looks only. The wheel and hub cap came off together whenever the need arose to remove a wheel. Even the spare wheel had a hub cap.

As roads were improved and people began to desire easier-riding cars, wheels were made smaller and smaller, and wooden wheels became obsolete. It then became the fashion for the wire or disc wheels to have the lug bolts in a smaller circle and the center of the wheel be made large enough so that the lug bolts were inside the smaller circle. The circle was given a lip onto which a larger hub cap snapped into place. Instead of having a hex shape, the outside of the snap-on hub cap was made in a half-moon style for smoothness and streamlining. The snap-on hub caps were made with the particular car maker's name or logo and were usually chrome plated.

To install one of the large hub caps, one set it in the opening of the wheel, held it was one hand, and then gave it a smack with the heel of the other hand to seat it on its spring clips. To remove it to gain access to the hub bolts, one pried it away from the wheel by using either the flat end of the lug wrench that came with the car or a wide, flat-blade screwdriver. A small cap was snapped into place on the front wheel hub to keep the wheel bearing grease in.

In the late 1940s it became fashionable to have the wheels almost completely covered with a stainless steel cover. There were spring clips on the outer edge of the cover, and they gripped the inside of the wheel rim. High-priced cars had them as standard equipment. My 1950 De-Soto, 1950 Chrysler, 1951 DeSoto, 1952 Mercury, 1955 Plymouth, 1969 Dodge Dart, 1969 Pontiac, 1973 Pontiac and 1983 Dodge station wagon all came factory equipped with them. A rubber hammer was required to install them. One had to take care when using the rubber hammer on the outer rim of the wheel cover to avoid denting it. One had to run one's finger around the edge of the wheel cover when installed to make sure all the spring clips were seating properly.

This car was factory equipped with an electrical device known as a "Startix." It was supposed to restart the engine automatically if the engine stalled. This device was available on several brands of automobiles, mostly in 1932, 1933 and 1934. Apparently it had some sort of expensive flaw as it was available for only a short time. I have never seen one on a car of that era that actually worked. Apparently a previous owner of this Franklin had the one on this car disconnected. When I bought this car it had a regular starter switch mounted on the toe board where the driver could step on the button with the right foot. Since the starter system worked properly while I had this car I let well enough alone and made no attempt to fix it or even to try to see why it did not work.

18 · 1949 Dodge

In the spring of 1959 my job required me to use my own car for company driving. I was reimbursed for mileage the same as the others who had later-model cars. I wanted to keep my 1950 DeSoto (#16) as a good car, and my 1933 Franklin (#17) was out of the question. I located a 1949 Dodge four-door sedan. It was one of the very early 1949 models that looked like a 1948 (also 1947 and 1946).

For some reason I never understood, Dodge kept side-opening hoods on its cars through these early 1949 models. It was the last Chrysler car to convert to front-opening hoods. When Chrysler modernized its cars for the 1949 model, all of them finally had front-opening hoods. The 1934 Chrysler and DeSoto had front-opening hoods and kept them for all the Airflow years. Chrysler and DeSoto kept the side-opening hoods for its non-Airflow, however.

Hudson had converted to front-opening hoods (from rear opening) for its big postwar change for its 1948 models and kept that style through the 1957 models, when the name Hudson no longer appeared on a new car. Buick also retained a type of side-opening hood. On the Buick the entire hood opened from one side or the other. With the aid of a helper the Buick hood could be completely removed from the car. If a 1941–1952 Buick happened to be in a hard enough accident, it was not unknown for the hood to fly off and land several feet away. Buick was the last car to convert to front-opening hoods.

Although the 1934 Chrysler and DeSoto were the first cars of modern times to have front-opening hoods, Stanley Steamer had them in 1903 and continued them until about 1918, when Stanley began equipping its cars with condensers at the front of the chassis. Then it converted to side-opening hoods like the rest of the U.S. auto industry.

Top: The author's 1949 Dodge (early). This early series was a carryover of the 1948 models. The later 1949 models were introduced a couple of months after this car was made.

Bottom: A 1952 Buick with its monstrous side-opening hood.

My car was the fancy model with factory radio, turn signals and the big heater/defroster. It had the standard transmission with fluid drive and the fenders were dented, but it ran well enough to use for company driving. I did not intend to grow old with this car but thought it would suit my purpose for the time being. I thought that by driving conservatively, not allowing the fluid drive to slip, I could get by. Had I realized how comparatively easy it was to remove the fluid drive unit and convert to standard, just like a Plymouth, I would have seriously considered doing so. Gas mileage was poor, however, and I stuck it out for about six months, when #19 became available, so I bought it and got rid of this car.

Another thing that helped convince me not to do any more on this car occurred when I had to have a front wheel cylinder overhauled. I was standing back watching the mechanic work when I noticed that the spindles, wheel bearings, and brake drums were different on each side. This implied that something bad had happened to this car already. Either it had been wrecked and improperly repaired with used parts or had a similar wheel bearing problem similar to the one in my 1950 De-Soto, #16. The paint seemed to be original on the entire car, however.

19 · 1948 Plymouth

A friend was going to sell his 1948 Plymouth four-door sedan, so I bought it and disposed of the 1949 Dodge (#18). My friend had maintained the car well for the five years or so he had owned it. The only drawback either of us knew about was the oil leak at the timing cover seal at the front of the engine. This friend was not mechanically inclined. His idea was that keeping the engine full of oil was sufficient and, since he did not know how to fix the leak himself, did not feel it was worth the money to pay a mechanic to fix it. Had I not been able to do the job myself I probably would not have spent the money to have it done professionally, either.

I also cleaned the oil from everything in sight and replaced the oil-soaked fan belt and radiator hoses while I had the engine apart. Replacing the seal was a simple matter of removing nuts and bolts, the radiator, the front engine mount, and so on, which was a rather routine but very dirty job, all done from above the car by reaching down. The timing chain and gears were okay with no "play."

With the radiator, fan, and front engine mount removed I had a clear view of the front frame horns, the very front end of the frame. To my dismay the left one was wrinkled, indicating that it had been bent and straightened out. One always wonders if such a thing gets straightened properly and if anything else could have been left unrepaired. Everything seemed to fit properly with no gaps or rattles. Both my friend and I had commented on how nice and shiny the front bumper was. Now we knew why: It had been replaced. My friend had not noticed anything unusual when he bought the car several years earlier, and no problems had developed while he drove it, so apparently there was nothing to be concerned about.

The author's 1948 Plymouth. Grille guard, extra driving lights and spotlight were all dealer-installed accessories.

Before the front timing cover can be removed to replace the seal, a puller is required to remove the harmonic balancer and crankshaft pulley. Although I would not be using that puller tool very often, I knew it would be a lot cheaper for me to buy the tool than to pay a mechanic to do the entire job. Using the puller took only a few minutes after the radiator, belts, and front engine mount were removed.

One day my employer needed a ride to the service station a few blocks away to pick up his car, which he had dropped off for routine servicing. He asked me if he could ride that far with me, knowing that I went right past the station on my way home. What else could I say except "yes"? He never let one of his cars get more than about two years old, so any car more than ten years old was almost like a horse and buggy to him. As I pulled into the station to let him out he remarked how well my Plymouth ran.

A fellow I knew had another car exactly like this one; the only difference between them was that his was light blue and mine was gray. We didn't live too far from each other, and, without realizing it at the time, each of us bought a pair of new Atlas snow tires from the same Standard Oil station. Somehow through the years I had acquired two extra Plymouth wheels which took 6.70 × 15 tires. I had already cleaned the wheels inside and out and painted them. Buying the tires and getting them installed was routine. The gas station man put them on the car and then put the regular rear tires, still on the wheels, in my trunk. This was about mid-November. Without realizing I had been there the other fellow went to the same station a few days later and bought two of the same brand and size tires as I had purchased, even down to the white sidewalls, like me.

As it turned out there was no snow that winter until March, when there were four deep snowfalls that one month. The snow tires on my car worked beautifully, as expected. Once when talking to this fellow I happened to mention how delighted I was with my new snow tires. He related just the opposite story. He was so disappointed with the performance of his snow tires on normal wet streets that he went back and made the station replace them after only about six weeks of normal driving. He said that the second set performed better than the original set. Neither of us could figure out how two sets of new tires could perform so differently on exactly the same make, model, and body style car, even to the point of coming from the same manufacturer, being the same size, and even being shipped to the same gas station.

About two years later the friend from whom I purchased this car indicated that he would like to buy it back, so I sold it back to him. As I recall the only expense, other than servicing, was the timing cover seal and gasket parts, which had cost only a few dollars; my labor had been my spare time.

As the photo shows, this car had a spotlight, extra fog/driving lights and a front bumper guard. I never had the occasion to use any of those extra lights, but they all worked. It was still possible in 1948 for a new car dealer to load up a car with accessories to raise his profit. New cars were still in demand for about the first half of the 1948 model year from the World War II days, when new cars were not being produced.

One of the few improvements made for the immediate postwar models was Chrysler's changing to dual wheel cylinders for the front brakes of all its 1946 cars. Basically, each front wheel brake had two wheel cylinders instead of one per wheel, as on its prewar cars and on all other U.S.-built cars.

Until the new system, when the driver stepped on the brake pedal, a single wheel cylinder was at the top of the backing plate, where the brake shoes were attached, and each end of the wheel cylinder pushed the top of one of the brake shoes, which rubbed against the inside of the brake drum, bolted to the wheel, to stop the car. On the dual system, there were two half-cylinders with just as much hydraulic pressure. Each half-cylinder actuated one brake shoe. One of the half-cylinders was located at about the three-o'clock position on the backing plate and the other at the nine-o'clock position.

The dual cylinder system was used only on the front wheels since they do most of the braking on every car. Servicing the brakes was the same as for the other type. The dual cylinder system was used until the early 1960s, when it was realized that power disc brakes were better in every way. All the Chrysler cars I had from 1948 through 1955 had the dual system. Chrysler was the only U.S. manufacturer to use this system.

20 · 1952 Mercury

In early 1961 had a chance to buy a recovered stolen car. The insurance company had bought the title to the car even though no one except the thief knew where the car was. When the police eventually found the car, they turned it over to the insurance company, where I worked at the time. I was able to buy the car for a little over junk price. I talked to the place where the police had it towed, and the man there told me that it ran okay and that I should have no trouble driving it the 50 miles from the storage lot to my home.

As strange as it may seem to us now, the Ford Motor Company was buying Hydramatic transmissions from General Motors for use in its Lincoln brand of cars. At the same time (1951–1952) Ford had its own brand of automatic transmission for its Ford and Mercury brands of cars. It called them Ford-O-Matic and Merc-O-Matic respectively. Each was a Ford copy of GM's Hydramatic that was changed just enough not to violate patents. General Motors also sold Hydramatics to independents Hudson and Kaiser as long as those two companies built those cars (into the mid 1950s).

The following Saturday I took a Greyhound bus to the storage lot and drove the car back with no trouble. It was a 1952 Mercury Monterey two-door hardtop with Merc-O-Matic. It was all white with dirt caked all over, inside and out. It also had blackwall tires, and the wheel covers were missing. Although for several months the car had been in the hands of the thief (who probably took no care of it at all and probably did nothing more than buy gasoline for it), I took a chance on buying it and also on driving it 50 miles back to my home with no idea, other than a phone conversation, whether it would make this trip without letting me down.

Top: The author's 1952 Mercury Monterey after arriving home from the recovery yard 50 miles away, near where a thief had abandoned it.

Bottom: The author's 1952 Mercury Monterey after it had been rubbed and scrubbed, wheels painted, wheel covers installed, and Port-A-Walls installed to make the tires look like white sidewalls.

The first thing I did was to scrub and scrub the car. I spent a couple of weekends just scrubbing. The inside came out presentable, and so did the outside paint. I bought a set of Port-A-Walls to dress up the black tires to look like white sidewalls; they had good tread. In the days before tubeless tires it was a simple matter to install Port-A-Walls. I located two pair of wheel covers, not exactly matching. I put one pair on the left side and the other pair on the right side. Now the car made a presentable appearance.

After about three months I was able to sell it for about $100 over the amount I had invested in it. The entire time I had the car I was on pins and needles wondering if it would stay running properly; it did. The car had the flathead V-8 engine and was not a tire-squealing performer but was adequate for what it was, and I had no mechanical problems with it at all.

I had no desire to keep a 1952 Mercury, especially a two-door hardtop, prone to squeaks and rattles; also, in those days, automatic transmissions were not all that trouble free, and I did not want to keep such a car any longer than it took to sell it. It was one of only two cars I bought with the sole purpose of trying to sell it for a profit.

This was the first car I owned that had a curved, one-piece windshield. General Motors introduced curved glass windshields for its 1949 models with its first major post-World War II modernization. There were two pieces of glass for the first few years, then the change was made to the one-piece style.

The early one-piece curved glass had trouble with distortion. The test was to park the car next to a brick wall or a clapboard house to see if looking through the windshield gave a straight or distorted view of the wall or house. Naturally, the curved glass was much more expensive to replace. By the mid-1950s the curved glass of the Ford and General Motors windshields wrapped around to the extent that it interfered with the door opening and made it difficult for the driver or passenger to enter or leave the front seat.

In 1952, when this Mercury was built, and for several years following, all of the side windows were still flat. Rear windows had been curved on several makes of U.S.-built cars since before World War II.

Mercury automobiles had been equipped with flathead V-8 engines since production began for the 1939 models, Mercury's first model. Although modified and improved during the ten model years since then (no 1943, 1944 or 1945 models had been produced), the flathead V-8 engine would be replaced by a much more modern overhead valve V-8 engine just two model years later, in 1954.

21 · *1955 Pontiac*

In May or June 1961 I was able to get a 1955 Pontiac medium series, four-door sedan for trade-in price from a fellow I knew. Although we both worked in the automobile business at the same place, his job was basically shuffling papers, and he had no contact with automobiles at all and little knowledge of how the different components functioned. Normal procedure was for him to ask me whenever he encountered a technical question, which wasn't often. He was about twenty years older than I was and had no real interest in taking care of the car himself. He would get a mechanical problem fixed as soon as he became aware that something was wrong. He would have the car washed occasionally.

The only drawbacks to the car were that the paint was dull, two-tone (green and tan), and it had fairly high mileage. I cleaned it up and brought the shine back to the paint and, without spending any money on it, sold it about three months later for about $125.00 more than I had in it. This car had power steering, brakes, and hydramatic. As with the 1952 Mercury (#20) I bought this car only with the idea of selling it. The owner knew I only wanted the car to sell at a profit. He was satisfied at getting his trade-in price and knew that the dealer from whom he was buying his new Pontiac would have made a profit on it. He would rather see me earn the profit than the dealer.

I was still leery of automatic transmissions and the expense when they got out of order. It would be another five years before I thought automatics were dependable enough to buy a used car with one. I didn't take to the idea of buying a car to resell. There was always the chance of breakdown and more expense. This was the last car I bought with the sole purpose of reselling at a profit.

This was the first year that Pontiac had a V-8 engine in modern times. From 1933 through its 1954 models a Pontiac could be purchased with either a six- or an eight-cylinder engine (the eight being a flathead straight eight). Oddly enough, in 1932 the Pontiac was given a flathead V-8 engine for that one year only. The Oakland name, which Pontiac replaced, had the V-8 engine in 1930 and 1931 only, its last year.

For the U.S. auto industry, 1955 was a banner year. Chevrolet introduced its first V-8 engine in modern times and so did Plymouth. All V-8s and most sixes now had overhead valve engines. Several makes of U.S. cars also switched from six-volt electrical systems to twelve volt to get more torque (power) to start their high-compression, V-8 engines. Several makes also switched the front suspension from king pins to ball joints. Almost all had modernized bodies, and a few had minor tail fins. Dual round headlights appeared on several medium- and high-priced cars. Most brands of U.S. cars finally had some type of automatic transmission available as well as power steering and brakes. The higher-powered V-8s were strong enough to easily run an air conditioner, but my Pontiac did not have one.

22 · 1938 Chrysler

In the summer of 1961 I was driving past the used car lot of a Lincoln Mercury dealer when I spotted a tall steel roof in the back row. It turned out to be a 1938 Chrysler Royal, a six-cylinder, four-door sedan. It was the sales manager's personal car, meaning that it did not belong to the dealership. The manager had acquired it to play with and was now tired of it. A price was agreed upon, and I wound up owning that car for eight years.

Although I eventually replaced the brakes, water pump, generator, starter, and tires, overhauled the engine, and did a few other things, this car never let me down. Often I would drive it when getting together with friends, and they would razz me about it. I would remind them that when I came in that 1938 Chrysler I was always on time. One of the friends was a police officer, and he would ask me (always when other people were around), "Do you have your 38 with you?" My answer would be, "Yes," and he would explain to the others that he meant my car, not a gun.

Chrysler made several major changes in all its cars for the 1937 models. One of the major ones was the engine. The Plymouth, Dodge, DeSoto and Chrysler lines each had a six-cylinder engine (Plymouth having the smallest, then Dodge). DeSoto and Chrysler had the same size, six-cylinder engine. Only the Chrysler brand also had an eight-cylinder line available. Although improved and modified through the years, the same basic six-cylinder engine was continued through the 1954 models, the last six-cylinder models offered by DeSoto or Chrysler.

The last year for the Chrysler Airflow was 1937; 1936 had been the last year for the DeSoto Airflow. For 1938 only, reasonably minor "facelift" changes had been made from the 1937 models. Many auto

The author's 1938 Chrysler with new paint, chrome redone, and white sidewall tires. The sealed-beam headlights do not show. The crown-mounted lights had amber lenses and were the turn signals, an accessory.

manufacturers did this through the years and still make facelifts from one model year to another periodically. For 1938 the six-cylinder Chrysler model was named "Royal," and, for the first time, the eight-cylinder model Chrysler was named "New York Special," later renamed "New Yorker." The New Yorker remained one of Chrysler's prestige models for decades. A spinoff of the New Yorker has been the "Fifth Avenue" model. Not to be outdone, Buick eventually named one of its high-priced models "Park Avenue."

At a flea market in Hershey, Pennsylvania, I found a brand new, still-in-the-original-box Southwind gasoline heater, complete with all the fittings and attachments, even the defroster fittings designed for that car. The hot water heater (with no defroster accommodation) that was in the car when I bought it was mediocre at best. As strange as it may seem, the rather undersized heater was the only accessory on the car. Although the dashboard had built-in defroster outlets to clear the windshield, that heater had no provision for connecting them. Until I hooked up the gasoline heater in 1961, they had gone unused for twenty-three years. Factory equipment of a horn ring, push-button starter button on the dashboard, two taillights, two sun visors, two arm rests, two windshield wipers, and so on which would have been accessories on lower-priced cars, were standard on all Chryslers.

That gasoline heater was every bit as nice as the one in my former 1936 Dodge (#10). In later January 1963 about twenty friends gathered one Sunday afternoon for cards and other table games. The temperature outside that day didn't get above about ten degrees all afternoon. About 4:00 PM everyone decided that they had had enough cards for the day, and we agreed to meet at a certain restaurant so we could get home early as we all had to work the next day.

The parking lot of the place where we had been playing cards was about ten feet below the street. My car started up right away as usual, and I turned on the gasoline heater as soon as the engine was running smoothly on fast idle. One of the other fellows stopped to ask directions, and the young lady riding with me rolled down the passenger door window to talk to him. He was stomping his feet on the ground and slapping his gloved hands together to try to stay warm. After about a minute he had the directions straight and went toward his own car, and she rolled the window back up.

When I saw that the fellow's car had started, I drove up the steep hill to go out onto the street. As I was waiting to pull out of the driveway onto the street, the young lady asked me if I could turn the heater down as it was burning her ankle. I immediately turned it to defrost and chuckled a little. She asked why I was chuckling. I told her that this was the coldest day of the season, and this was the oldest car there; the other cars would not be producing heat from their heaters for at least ten minutes. We sat there a full minute with the window rolled down to give directions. We were not even out of the driveway when she said she was still getting too much heat. I think she understood why I was chuckling.

In April 1963 I heard of an old Chrysler dealership that had a bunch of obsolete parts, parts books, shop manuals, and so forth. The place had recently changed hands, and these items were in the way. I was able to buy everything at a very friendly price. A worm-and-sector shaft for the steering, a new engine oil pump, a new windshield wiper transmission mechanism for each side, a new wiper motor, a new temperature gauge, two new horn rings, new pistons and valves for the engine, new trunk hinges, a new headlight switch, and other such goodies I was able to sell. Everything was new-in-the-box, genuine MoPar.

On my various other travels I found a brand-new trunk lid and more other new parts than I can recall now. I learned that the trunk hinges were a weak spot of the car as they were outside mounted and made of basically chrome-plated pot metal. In addition to the new pair with the parts from the old Chrysler dealer I found four more hinges. Eventually all of them broke, one at a time, and when I sold the car the last two I had were on it.

Another weak spot was the headlight switch. I tried to always have at least one on hand as I never knew when one was going to fall apart. Besides Chrysler, the same headlight switch was also used on certain Plymouth, Dodge and DeSoto cars.

Once, when I had a later-model, ignition key-starter switch, I found that it would fit exactly where the original lock had been with no alterations and would keep the same appearance. The only things to do were (1) to transfer the original lock cylinder to the later-model switch so I could continue to use the same key, and (2) to transfer the wires from the original start switch on the dashboard to the later switch. I left the original start switch in place just for looks, but it was no longer connected to anything.

After driving and enjoying this car for about five years and having it in excellent mechanical condition and with new white sidewall tires, I decided to have the chrome replated and the car painted.

As with many cars of the 1930s, the safety glass laminate started to get foggy, especially around the edges. The company where I worked had dealings with an auto glass company. Before having the car painted I removed the windshield and all four door glasses, the two front vent windows and the two side quarter windows and took them to the auto glass company's shop with instructions that I was in no special hurry to get them back. They used my project as "fill in" work they could do when no regular customers were waiting for their cars. After about three weeks everything was ready. Since these were all flat windows and each had to be cut to an exact size, I was somewhat apprehensive about whether everything would fit correctly and go back together properly. My apprehension was wasted as everything fit perfectly. The new glass made quite an improvement in the general appearance of the car.

I removed all the chrome and also the stainless steel door side moldings and handles. I realized that having the moldings and handles off would keep dust down and make for a better paint job in general. All the chrome parts came back looking absolutely like new. I sanded the car down with 220 wet and ended with 400 wet sandpaper. I had also regrained the inside garnish moldings.

Until the mid-1950s many cars had a full garnish molding completely surrounding each window inside the car, held in place with screws. The molding was finished in some kind of woodgrain decal to match the woodgrain-appearing decal on the dashboard. In normal driving, with windows rolled down in nice weather (since cars were not air conditioned before the mid-1950s), elbows were put on the garnish moldings. After a few years the woodgrain wore off.

Regraining was not as difficult as many people suspect. Basically, it required removing the moldings from inside the car, sanding them down smooth and then spraying on whichever light color was correct. After letting the moldings dry thoroughly, the appropriate dark color was applied with a piece of cheesecloth with one stroke in one direction; then this was left to dry thoroughly. To make everything match I removed every garnish molding and regrained them all at the same time.

When the body shop saw how much work I had done to prepare the surface, they gave it one of the slickest, shiniest paint jobs I have ever seen: nice and glossy baked enamel with no dirt, no runs, no fisheyes, and no orange peel. It was the original dark blue nonmetallic. When I reassembled everything (being careful to avoid scratches) it turned out to be a real head turner and smile encourager with many oohs and aahs.

At another Hershey flea market I found a sealed beam conversion kit with all the necessary parts and instructions. Converting to sealed beams meant removing the original factory headlight lens, reflector, and wiring and installing the sealed beam kit. Sealed beams improved night driving considerably and do not detract from the appearance of the car. I also added small front lights with amber lenses as turn signals, using the same type of add-on signal switch as the 1946 Hudson (#12). I also added red signal lights on the sides of the trunk for safety.

Eventually I overhauled the engine and, without changing the outward appearance of anything, I replaced the intake and exhaust manifolds, cylinder head, distributor assembly, generator, voltage regulator, and other items from later-model engines to give a little more power and smoothness.

I sold this car only because I had owned it for eight years, had it in excellent condition and was tired of it. The complete set of parts books and the shop manual went with the car as did all the parts I had not replaced.

23 · *1955 Plymouth*

In 1962, after disposing of my 1950 DeSoto (#16), I found a 1955 Plymouth four-door sedan, six cylinder with standard transmission, on a used car lot. It was the middle line Savoy. At this time automatic transmissions were still a long way from trouble free, and I would rather go through the inconvenience of shifting gears by hand than live with the constant uncertainty that a big repair bill could hit at any time. This car had been freshly painted and made a very nice appearance. It also ran very well and had almost new tires. It did not have a radio, but I located one in a junkyard and installed it. At the time, stereo systems and even FM radios were not available for cars, only standard AM.

Whoever did the painting did an excellent job sanding and spraying but not a good job masking. I spent a couple weekends removing things such as headlight doors, the hood ornament, the taillights, and various handles and moldings and cleaning off the paint from the edges and reinstalling them.

The first year that Plymouth and most of the rest of the U.S. auto industry had pedals suspended from under the dashboard instead of protruding through the floor (as they had for the previous fifty years) was 1955. I don't know exactly what Plymouth did or did not do, but they just didn't get it right. The pedals were too high off the floor, plus I couldn't step squarely on the pedal with the ball of my shoe without the toe of the shoe touching the bracket on which the pedal was attached. I tried adjusting the front seat to different positions, but that did not help. I never understood why cars with automatic transmission and power brakes had the brake pedal in the correct position, but the standard transmission cars without power brakes did not. This

The author's 1955 Plymouth Savoy.

inability to get used to this "dangling pedal" arrangement was the chief reason I sold this car.

In addition to the dangling pedals, Plymouth, the rest of the Chrysler Corporation, and the rest of the U.S. auto industry made many major changes for their 1955 models. Even outside door handles were improved, making the doors much easier to open, especially when you had an armload of bundles.

The six-cylinder engine was the same basic design Plymouth had been using since its 1937 models although it had been modified and improved through the years. It was destined to remain in use through Plymouth's 1959 models. Plymouth also introduced a V-8 engine (a first for them), although Chrysler, DeSoto and Dodge each already had a V-8. That year, 1955, was also the first V-8 for Chevrolet since 1919. Furthermore, it was an excellent sales year for the entire U.S. auto industry. Ford and Chevrolet also introduced updated and modernized cars. Personally, I preferred the Plymouth although Chevrolet and Ford outsold Plymouth.

This car was very dependable and rode very nicely in the year I owned it. The only repair, if it can be called that, I ever made was to install the radio, its aerial, and its electrical suppressors.

When a young fellow answered my newspaper ad and came to see the car I took him for a ride down a nearby very long and steep hill with a curve about half way. As we neared the bottom of the hill I checked my mirrors to make sure no one was following, then took both hands off the steering wheel and stepped on the brake pedal. The car stopped quickly, quietly, and in a perfectly straight line, as I knew it would. I then told the prospective buyer that I was going to turn around and go back up that same hill in high gear. A look of skepticism come over his face. The slight run I had for the hill was erased halfway up when I had to slow down for the curve, but the car picked right up and made it smoothly and effortlessly over the top.

The young fellow then took the wheel and drove around the neighborhood streets to get the feel of the car and enjoy it more. He had driven to see my car in a 1950 Ford with a flathead, six-cylinder engine, a rather rare car itself. He was undecided whether to spend money making necessary repairs to his Ford or to get another car. He decided to buy my car and gave me a deposit. When he came back the next day to bring me the balance of the money and take the car, he told me that the ride up the steep hill in high gear was what had convinced him to buy my car, even if he had to pay my asking price, which he did.

This was the first car I owned that was factory equipped with tubeless tires. The entire U.S. auto industry switched to tubeless tires in 1955. Although I did not buy this car until 1962 I had an opportunity to go through the Chevrolet assembly plant in Norwood, Ohio, in 1955.

One of the procedures I observed was the installing of the tires on the wheels. It took the installer only a few seconds to pick up a wheel coming along the conveyor belt, dip it in a slippery soaplike solution, lay it flat on the tire machine, then install a valve in the wheel and lock it in. Then he would pick up a tire from the other conveyor belt and shove it part way onto the wheel. Next the man pulled a lever which caused the other section of the machine to lower, and he would push the tire the rest of the way onto the slippery wheel, wrap around the tread of the tire, and seat the tire on the wheel. Finally, the man held the air hose up to the valve to fill it with air.

The entire operation did not take more than about fifteen seconds. The longest part of the entire operation was holding the air hose to the tire valve and filling the tire with air. From this observation it was easy to see why the car makers liked tubeless tires; they didn't have to purchase or bother with inner tubes. Besides taking longer to install, there was always the chance that an inner tube would be pinched during installation.

Training people in dealerships and at tire stores took a little time as did getting tire repair and installation machines to everyone. Leak problems were few and far between. I never had any problems with the twelve cars I owned with tubeless tires.

24 · *1940 Chrysler*

Shortly after I found the 1955 Plymouth (#23) in 1962 I located a 1940 Chrysler from a private owner. It was the Windsor series, four-door sedan with the six-cylinder engine and, of course, no fluid drive. Its fenders and two of its doors were dented, but the two-tone green upholstery was unbelievably clean. In 1940 only Chrysler cars had plain fenders; the Plymouth, Dodge and DeSoto brands all had what they called "speed lines" in the fender metal. These speed lines gave every car a distinctive appearance as they were different on each of the three brands of cars. It was a nightmare for a body man to repair a dented speed line fender.

I was not especially looking for this car, but I knew that I would probably sell the 1955 Plymouth because of the dangling pedals I could not get used to, so I bought this 1940 Chrysler because it was available.

In 1939 Chrysler Corporation and most of the rest of the U.S. auto industry first placed the gearshift on the steering column and did away with the "stick" in the middle of the floor. The emergency brake handles were relocated to under the dashboard in easy reach of the driver. The exact location varied from manufacturer to manufacturer. For the 1940 models all the Chrysler cars kept the same gearshift mechanism arrangement inside the steering column. Sometimes the linkage would get out of adjustment. The only trouble I had with this car was on two occasions when it would not come out of low gear. The first time I was able to adjust the linkage, but the second time I had to take the car to a mechanic, who had to remove the transmission to repair the levers inside, so he said. In any case it gave no more trouble as long as I owned the car.

In addition, the 1940 model year brought many changes in the entire U.S. auto industry. All manufacturers switched to sealed beam

The author's 1940 Chrysler Windsor.

headlights where the lens, bulb and reflector were all made in one piece. These were a tremendous improvement over the old-style headlights. Chrysler made tremendous improvements in its complete line of cars, from the lowest-priced Plymouth to the highest-priced Chrysler. The cars were now very streamlined; the doors had rotary latches, making them close a lot easier and a lot more firmly. The seats were much deeper and much more comfortable. Springs, shock absorbers, and the chassis had been redesigned to give the car a much smoother ride. On the four-door sedan models the rear doors were enormous and very easy to enter and leave. These cars were highly regarded by taxicab companies well into the 1950s, primarily because the huge rear doors made it very easy for cab passengers to enter and leave.

On one occasion I was at a picnic one Sunday afternoon when a summer thunderstorm approached. Someone had brought a big wash tub, ice, and a half keg of beer. One of the picnicking couples lived fairly close to the park and quickly invited everyone to their basement to continue the picnic. No one wanted to remove the tap from the beer keg as the beer would have gone flat. There were no pickup trucks or vans there, only regular passenger cars, and no one's trunk was big enough to hold the wash tub, keg, and tap as a complete unit.

I volunteered the use of the rear floor of my 1940 Chrysler sedan. I opened both rear doors. One fellow took one of the wash tub handles, and another fellow took the opposite handle. The first fellow walked completely through the car and out the other side, and both set the wash tub down in the middle of the floor. It was a perfect fit between the front and rear seats.

At the couple's house the procedure was reversed, and everyone made it inside a few seconds before the cloudburst started, and the beer tap did not have to be reinstalled. I drove slowly and tried to avoid all bumps and anything that would shake the keg any more than absolutely necessary. From what I understand, the first couple of draws from that keg were pretty fierce.

Except for the dented fenders this car appeared to have original paint, and it polished up well. I would have liked to have the fenders and door repaired properly, but I just couldn't bring myself to spend the money, knowing that I would probably not get it back.

For several months I had noticed the clutch taking hold closer and closer to the floor. I adjusted it and noticed that there was not too much adjustment remaining. When I had had the car about three and one half years, one evening I heard a strange knock in the engine for a few seconds, then the inside of the car filled with smoke and smelled like hot oil. The engine would still run, so I presumed that a piston had come apart. I drove the car home and parked it. A few days later, in 1965, I located a 1962 Dodge Lancer four-door sedan; this was the same basic car as the Plymouth Valiant. I traded the 1940 Chrysler in on the 1962 Dodge Lancer and was glad to get the $50.00 trade-in allowance.

By some strange coincidence the 1938 Chrysler four-door sedan (#22) and this 1940 Chrysler Windsor four-door sedan had "2664" as the last four digits of the serial number. I don't have any idea what the odds are for such a thing happening, especially since both cars were purchased used, eighteen months apart, when each was over twenty years old at the time. I have heard of such things happening in large fleets that own thousands of cars from different manufacturers. Perhaps someone with a "Jimmy the Greek" inclination could determine the production runs of each of those models and estimate the likelihood that they would wind up in the hands of different owners in the same city, and then that the same individual would wind up buying both of them.

This car had a fairly minor problem that I would have liked to fix myself if I had had the time. During a medium or heavy rain the windshield would leak. Like all Chrysler cars of this era, it had a flat, two-piece windshield with a divider strip down the middle separating the right and left sides. There was a chrome reveal molding on the outside and a garnish molding on the inside. It takes a special tool to remove the outer reveal molding without damaging it and/or cracking the windshield glass. That left applying clear sealer to the outside, then removing the inside garnish moldings and applying more sealer. Neither worked. The next step would have been to buy the special tool. Unfortunately, the engine problem reared its ugly head before I had a chance to do that.

The year that Walter P. Chrysler passed away, 1940, was an important year for the Chrysler Corporation. He became ill in 1935 and retired, then lingered for another five years.

His earlier jobs were in the railroad industry, starting at the very bottom and working his way up until, by 1910, he was in charge of a large railroad repair facility in Pittsburgh. After a big corporate shakeup in General Motors in 1910, Charles W. Nash became president of GM and picked Walter Chrysler to head its Buick division manufacturing operations in 1911. In 1915 William C. Durant again took control of GM. He and Chrysler had one disagreement too many and Chrysler resigned.

After a short period of idleness Chrysler was approached by Willys-Overland (W-O) of Toledo, which was having financial problems. Its chief products were the low-priced Overland and the medium-priced Willys-Knight. He had a contract with W-O for two years at one million dollars a year. He was able to do what he was hired to do, and then Maxwell-Chalmers approached him. Chrysler told them that his contract with W-O would be over soon, so he could take on Maxwell-Chalmers's problems.

Instead of a large salary, Chrysler asked for big stock options. One of Maxwell's problems that caused sales to drop was a poor rear axle mounting. Chrysler had the mounting redesigned, then lowered the price of the Maxwell so that the company made only $5.00 per car profit on each car. The lower prices boosted sales. Chrysler had wanted a car with his own name on it for a long time. At Maxwell-Chalmers he achieved that end.

25 · *1938 Chrysler*

About a year after I bought the 1938 Chrysler Royal sedan (#22) I found a 1938 Chrysler Royal three-passenger coupe being driven by a college student. It was running on between four and five cylinders, presumably because some valves were burned and leaking compression. The brakes also pulled. He let it go for junk price. Since it ran so poorly I did not drive it except to the garage I was renting. I made no attempt to fix the engine or brakes because I was not going to keep the car. My plan was to remove everything I could use for the four-door sedan and scrap the rest.

Beginning in the mid-1930s the most beautifully streamlined cars made by every U.S. auto manufacturer were the three-passenger coupes. With only one seat in the car, the rear of the body was very graceful, with its gentle slope to the rear. By that time windshields and the rear windows, as part of the roof, on all cars were slanted.

The trunks were cavernous. Since there was no rear seat, there was no quarter panel or rear seat upholstery. This allowed the price of the three-passenger coupe to be the lowest of any body style. Some car models offered a rumble seat as late as 1939, but these had pretty much lost their appeal by that time. The real streamlined three-passenger coupes were available as late as the 1948 models of Ford and Chrysler. The three-passenger coupe was also an ideal car for a salesperson who had to carry bulky sample cases in addition to personal baggage while traveling.

I had removed most of what I had planned to remove when someone broke into the rented garage where I had the car stored and took a wheel with a very good 6.00 × 16 tire and some other small things of no value to anyone else. I was able to save the transmission which, it

146

The author's 1938 Chrysler coupe.

turned out, I never needed and gave to the man who eventually purchased the four-door sedan (#22) along with other things. As soon as
the theft occurred I called a junkyard to haul away what remained. I
had that car only about three months.

26 · 1950 Chrysler

In early 1965 I had the chance to buy a 1950 Chrysler four-door sedan with the six-cylinder engine and the fluid drive, semiautomatic transmission. I knew the transmission was bad but decided to buy the car for its engine as it was the same basic engine used in the 1938 and 1940 Chryslers I already owned. For the twenty-fifth anniversary of the first Chrysler car in 1949, Chrysler revamped its entire line of automobiles. For the 1950 models facelifts were made and considerably improved the looks of all the 1950 models over the 1949s. The entire line of Chrysler cars kept the same basic body style from the 1949 through the 1952 models.

Although my 1950 had the six-cylinder engine, the year model 1950 was the last year Chrysler had a straight-eight-cylinder engine available. For the 1951 model Chrysler introduced its V-8 engine, known as the "hemi" because of its hemispherical-shaped combustion chambers. This engine design was of great interest in the U.S. auto industry at the time. For 1952 a slightly smaller version of this V-8 was available in the DeSoto, and for 1953 Dodge was given its version of it.

Except for the grille, bumpers, dashboard, and the fluid drive transmission this car was almost identical to my 1950 DeSoto (#16). My plan was to use the engine in either the 1938 or the 1940 while the original of either was being rebuilt whenever either would need it. I would part out and eventually junk the 1950. My plans did not materialize, however, as I was transferred unexpectedly about 100 miles away. To further complicate matters, the property on which the carriage house I had been renting was located had been sold, and I had to vacate it quickly. With none of my plans for it realized and with no time to remove any of the useable parts I had wanted to remove, I junked the 1950 Chrysler after having had it just a couple of months.

27 · *1962 Dodge*

The responsibilities of my job transfer and promotion left me less time to work on and tinker with old cars. When the 1940 Chrysler (#24) collapsed with the bad engine I decided to get a slant six Chrysler four-door sedan. I had heard only good things about the slant six with the automatic transmission. The 1962 Dodge Lancer was my first direct experience with a slant six with automatic transmission.

History was to prove my faith justified as this slant six engine saved Chrysler from going under in the 1960s. The big V-8 Chrysler and Dodge (and DeSoto) engines had been bombs, the cars were ugly and awkward, and sales dropped.

The flathead, six-cylinder engine had been around almost thirty years (since 1933), although improved and modified along the way. The flathead six had been made in various sizes for the entire Chrysler line, including Dodge trucks.

The slant six proved to be just as dependable, appearing in various models of Plymouth, Chrysler, Dodge and Dodge trucks from 1960 through 1987. This 1962 Dodge Lancer, the same basic car as the Plymouth Valiant, was the first of eight cars I would eventually own with the slant six and automatic transmission. I was delighted with the way this car drove, even though it was a "compact" car. This was my first experience owning a modern car (four years old) since the 1951 DeSoto (#14) I had purchased in 1955, when the car was five years old.

One of the idiosyncrasies of this car was that the heater system would not switch from heat to defrost or back again. I considered this a relatively minor problem, nor worthy of spending a large amount of money to fix. I merely moved everything manually to defrost and

The author's 1962 Dodge Lancer, the same basic car as the Plymouth Valiant.

blocked the linkage there. Because I considered the defrost mode to be more important than the heat, things worked out fine. Either in conjunction with or because of this problem, the hot water valve would not shut off. This meant that hot water was always running through the heater core. After the first balmy day or two in the spring I would disconnect both heater hoses from the heater core and connect them to a piece of plain pipe to bypass the heater core for the summer until the nippy days of autumn arrived.

Another idiosyncrasy of these cars was the tires. They were size 6.50 × 13, then B78 × 13, and what I learned is that you should not balance them. I had the fronts balanced before going out of town one weekend. One of the weights came off each wheel. When I took the car back to where I had them balanced, the mechanic balanced them again, at no charge. The following weekend the same thing happened; again they were rebalanced at no charge to me.

A few weeks later I made another weekend trip, but, when I found that other weights had come off, I did not go back for another rebalance. Instead I removed all the remaining weights and nothing happened: no vibration, no strange tire wear. For as long as I owned that car I never had the tires balanced again, even when I had to get new tires. This was true on all the slant six compacts I had with 13-inch tires. The slant six automatics I had with 14-inch and 15-inch tires needed normal balancing, however.

Eventually it came time to replace the ball joints. I learned that only the lowers wear on slant six compacts. I did not have tools or experience with them, so I had them replaced professionally. When Chrysler began using torsion bars in 1957, it did not get everything right, and broken torsion bars were not unusual. By the 1960 slant six compact era Chrysler had gotten its act together, and broken torsion bars became virtually unknown.

As with the flathead, six-cylinder Chryslers of the 1930s, 1940s and 1950s, I learned the soft spots of the slant six cars. I always tried to keep on hand alternator brushes, a water pump, a voltage regulator, a tail pipe, and, when possible, a starter with a good bendix drive and a complete working alternator. All of those items would let you know ahead of time that they were going bad so you could plan ahead.

Once, when driving through a big city on the interstate during a heavy rainstorm, with wipers and defroster going and lights on, I noticed that the alternator gauge was showing discharge. I had to go completely through the city and about 10 miles out in the country before I found a place to stop under an overpass. I shut everything off except the engine, then got out and raised the hood. The problem was that the green wire connector had come loose from the back of the alternator. Plugging it back in solved the problem. I stayed there with everything still off and ran the engine at fast idle for about ten minutes, then continued on with no more trouble.

One day, while I was driving in town in the rain, the left windshield wiper stopped cleaning. It still moved across the windshield, but the blade was not pressing on the glass hard enough to clean the glass. It seems that the coil spring inside the wiper arm assembly had rusted away and broken. When I got home I switched the good spring from the right side to the left one. MoPar did not have the springs available separately. Eventually I located a spring that worked well enough for the right arm until I found a set of very good arms at a junkyard to replace them. I added this to the list of items to always keep on hand.

Another time on another interstate I was riding along at the speed limit at the time, 70 mph, when the engine suddenly developed a dead miss. Since I could see a gas station sign a couple of miles away so and there was no knocking noise, I decided to continue that far. I pulled to an out-of-the-way spot in the station before shutting off the engine. When I raised the hood I found the #2 spark plug wire flopping around loose. I reconnected it, pushed all the other plug wires in firmly at both the spark plug end and the distributor cap end to make sure none was loose, and then closed the hood.

I walked around to the young attendant and asked him if he could clean one spark plug for me. He said "No," that all he could do was to sell me a new set of spark plugs. Realizing that the only reason the engine was missing was that the #2 spark plug was fouled with gasoline and oil, I did not want to pay drug store price for new spark plugs I really didn't need. I knew that reconnecting the wire to the spark plug would cause electricity to flow through and ignite the accumulated fuel and oil and that it would soon be working again properly. I said "No, thank you" to the attendant. I knew that in about a mile or two of driving back on the interstate the miss would be gone, which it was.

In the autumn of 1968 this car's paint was getting bad, and I did not want it to go through another winter. I took it to the same Earl Scheib where I had had the 1938 Chrysler sedan, #22, painted. I sanded it down myself before taking it to them. This Lancer turned out very nice but not as nice as the 1938 Chrysler.

When this car reached 80,000 miles in late 1969 the engine began smoking a little. I then learned that someone I knew well was going to trade in a 1960 Valiant slant six automatic with 29,000 miles for a more up-to-date car. The body was badly rusted, but I knew the mileage to be correct. I was able to get the car for the trade-in price of $150.00. As the 1962 Lancer started to smoke more I decided to switch engine and transmission assemblies, so the Lancer wound up with a 29,000-mile engine and transmission. Neither of those units gave me any problems as long as I kept that car.

One weekend I rented a cherry picker (portable crane) and drove the 1960 Valiant into the garage. After removing the hood, radiator and hoses, battery, air cleaner, and so on it was a simple matter of removing the drive shaft and engine mounts and then disconnecting the carburetor linkage, fuel lines, wiring, transmission control cable, and so forth. Then it was a matter of wrapping the chain around the manifolds securely and lifting the engine and transmission assembly high enough to clear the tops of the fenders and grille. Next, since the cherry picker was on wheels, I simply rolled it aside and lowered everything to the garage floor on some wooden blocks to keep the slanted engine from tipping over on its side. Then I pushed the 1960 Valiant out of the garage, drove the 1962 Lancer into the garage and repeated the process. Finally I hooked the cherry picker up to the 1960 Valiant engine and transmission assembly and basically reversed the process, putting it into the 1962 Lancer. I completed everything in one weekend. By Sunday night muscles I never knew I had were aching. There was a Dodge dealer about 3 miles away, and I took the car there to get them to adjust the transmission linkage correctly with the special tool for that purpose.

By mid-1971 a corporate change had sent me to the Deep South, where year-round air conditioning was required. By that time the Lancer showed over 115,000 miles, and I reluctantly junked it just before moving.

28 · *1960 Plymouth*

The lady from whom I bought this car had recently retired and had the money to buy a new 1969 Valiant. She did not want to be seen as a little old lady driving a little old car. She was unable to take care of a car herself and did not have it washed as often as it got dirty. The result was that dirt remained on the car long enough to allow rust to form. The car stood outside before she retired from her job. The best thing about the car was the 29,000 actual miles on the odometer.

My hope was to restore this car and be able to drive it for several years. The 1960 and 1961 Valiants were the same except for a slight difference in the way the grilles were painted.

As I got more into the idea of restoring the low-mileage 1960, I began to realize that too much cutting and welding would be involved, and I did not have the tools or equipment to cut and weld. Having the rust repaired at a body shop would have cost more than the car would be worth in the foreseeable future. About this time I decided to switch engines and transmission with #27, the 1962 Dodge Lancer. When that was completed I saved the mechanical parts that could be used on the Lancer and then junked this 1960 Valiant. I wound up paying $150 for a 29,000-mile engine, transmission and some other parts, which is better than I could have done at a junkyard for such low-mileage parts.

In 1960 General Motors, Ford and Chrysler all came out with compact cars to counter the small foreign cars. Hudson had already made its Hudson Jet, which was a good enough car, but the company was having corporate financial problems and just couldn't get enough production to succeed. Studebaker eventually produced a low-priced car. It was based on its low-priced Lark and called the Scotsman. It was almost devoid of chrome, and even the hub caps were painted instead

154

The author's 1960 Valiant with 29,000 miles, from the original lady owner.

of being chrome or stainless steel. The Scotsman turned out to be just too "plain Jane" to sell.

The low-priced Lark models were nicknamed Larkabaker, and the higher-priced Hawks were nicknamed Hawkabaker. Of the Ford Falcon, the Chevrolet Corvair and the Plymouth Valiant, the Valiant was, by far, the best.

Between the Corvair's air-cooled engine problems and its tendency to roll over, it got a bad name from the start. It is what propelled attorney Ralph Nader to fame with his book *Unsafe at Any Speed.* The rear-mounted Corvair engine plus the swing axle rear suspension tended to make the car whip around sideways and roll over because drivers were not used to the weight of the engine being in the rear of the car instead of the front. The inherent flaws of an air-cooled engine are that the cylinders are opposed to each other and have a tendency to leak oil and overheat.

The Ford Falcon was somewhat underpowered because its engine was so small. The Valiant did not have any of the Corvair's or Falcon's problems. It had an alternator to keep the battery charged instead of the then out-of-date generator system. It also had a correctly sized engine with adequate power and a good three-speed automatic transmission operated by push buttons and was, in general, more up to date.

The Valiant was so well received in 1960 that the same basic car was given to Dodge dealers for 1961 and 1962 as the Dodge Lancer, and the 1960 Valiant was continued unchanged for 1961. Later, this slant six engine was put into the half-ton truck as well as full size Dodge and Chrysler cars.

29 · *1961 Plymouth*

This was the 1961 Valiant four-door sedan that I bought strictly as a parts car to help restore the 1960 Valiant (#28). This car was no cream puff by any stretch of the imagination. The engine and transmission had already been removed by the previous owner, who had no more use for the rest of the car. The sheet metal on the body was in surprisingly good condition with no rust or dents. The paint was awful but that didn't matter.

Since my original plans of restoring the 1960 Valiant were not going

The author's 1961 Valiant, from which some usable parts were removed for the 1962 Lancer.

to pan out I junked this car after removing what body parts I thought I might eventually use on the 1962 Lancer (#27). I junked the 1960 Valiant, now with no engine or transmission, and the 1961 Valiant, also with no engine or transmission, plus the engine and transmission that were removed from the 1962 Lancer. When the junk man came to get everything he was surprised at what was there but took everything without complaining.

May they rest in pieces.

30 · *1967 Plymouth*

While at an old car show in a town about 50 miles from home one Sunday, I found this 1967 Valiant on the local Ford dealer's used car lot. It was a four-door sedan, slant six automatic with 27,000 miles showing on the odometer. The mileage agreed with the condition of the rest of the car. Since I knew I would be needing a car with air conditioning soon, I reasoned that this car would be worth getting a "hang on" unit installed.

The Ford dealer was not open on Sunday, so I called the next day and drove there again that evening to test drive the car. The lone salesman stuck a dealer license plate on the back of the car and let me take it for a test drive without coming along himself.

As I was driving along one of the country roads outside of town I saw a state trooper pass me in the opposite direction. I then noticed in my mirror that he had turned around and was following me. Sure enough he pulled me over. He wanted me to know that one of the headlights was out. He had seen the dealer license plate on the rear and knew to whom it was issued. He wrote out a warning form to the dealer and gave it to me to give to the dealer.

When I returned to the dealership used car lot and gave the salesman the warning form, he apologized all over the place for whoever was supposed to have inspected this car for such things before placing it on the used car lot for sale. He said that he would see to it that the headlight was fixed, regardless of whether I decided to buy the car. I had already decided to buy it. I gave him a deposit and arranged to return the next evening by Greyhound bus to complete the sale, pay him the balance of the money and drive the car home. The first thing the salesman said when he saw me was that he had given the warning notice about the headlight to the service manager first thing in the morning. The manager assured the salesman that it would be fixed right away.

After the formalities and paper signing were completed and it was time for me to drive home, I noticed that the car was parked in the exact same spot where I had parked it the previous night. I turned on the lights and only one headlight came on. The salesman was furious because such a simple thing had not been fixed, especially after getting a police warning about it. He assured me that someone's head was going to roll. I told him that such a thing was not necessary as I could replace a sealed beam myself at home the next day. He was grateful for my understanding. After searching for the parts department keys for about ten minutes he was able to get in and find its stock of sealed beams. He gave me one and I kept it on the front seat during my ride home in case that same trooper, or another officer, stopped me. No one did and I replaced the headlight myself the next day.

Shortly after I acquired the car, Sears automotive stores offered a friendly price for its hang-on air conditioning unit. It was not as efficient as the factory installed unit, but it was acceptable. I had it installed in the spring of 1971, making sure I got all the warranty papers.

The car performed reasonably well, and I made a couple of weekend trips to see whether any kinks needed attention. Sometimes the car was hard to start and loaded up with gasoline. I removed the carburetor and took it to a garage nearby for overhaul. I reinstalled it the next evening as I was planning another trip out of town the following weekend. The trip to visit friends went fine until almost 20 miles from home Sunday night on the way home. The first 280 miles had gone fine, but then the carburetor loaded up with gasoline and stopped running on the interstate, but I was able to coast off the road.

After about half an hour a state trooper stopped to investigate. He had his dispatcher call a tow truck with a mechanic. The mechanic was able to fix the car without towing it in (the needle valve in the carburetor had come loose). He was sympathetic, but I still had to pay for a Sunday night service call. He wrote on the receipt exactly what he had done. When I took the receipt back to the garage where the carburetor was overhauled I was given a refund.

A couple of months later I moved to the Deep South. After about a month the air conditioner stopped cooling. Armed with the warranty papers I went to the nearest Sears automotive store, where they located a loose freon hose clamp, allowing freon to escape. Repairs were made at

The author's 1967 Valiant shortly after having all the rust repaired and having been painted light green.

no cost to me. About three months later it stopped cooling again. This time they found a bad expansion valve and replaced it at no charge to me.

While still under the Chrysler five year/50,000 mile warranty this car developed a burned intake valve. It was replaced at a Chrysler-Plymouth dealer at no charge to me, but I decided to have the rest of the valves ground at the same time to ensure that the entire engine would run smoothly and evenly for a long time at a savings in labor to me since they already had the cylinder head off to replace the burned valve. Of the eight slant six automatic Dodge and Plymouth cars I owned, this was the only one where the head had to be removed; an oil pan was never removed.

On two separate occasions the same unusual thing happened on this car. I went to rotate tires when one of the lugs in a front brake drum stripped and would not loosen. This meant that I could not get the wheel off. Fortunately for me this did not occur either time when I had a flat tire. The only solution was quite time consuming. It meant removing the front outer wheel bearing, which would allow the brake drum with the wheel and tire to come off as a complete assembly.

I laid the assembly down in the driveway and took a hammer and chisel to the nut of the stripped bolt until it broke. It was not possible to get a grip on the head of the stripped bolt inside the brake drum. After a very frustrating time the offending nut would finally crack or break apart enough to come off. Since there were five lug nuts and bolts holding on each wheel, it was not unsafe to drive around town with only four, temporarily.

The next step was to take the drum in question to an auto parts store with a press. Although only one bolt was stripped I had all five pressed out to avoid this happening again on the same drum. This happened on each front drum. I made sure the machine shop pressed only right thread bolts in on the drum where right thread bolts were pressed out (also right thread nuts for those bolts) and left thread nuts and bolts for the opposite side. I would not let anyone take a cutting torch and burn off the stripped nut as the heat from the torch would certainly take the temper out of the brake drum or hub, making them warp or eventually crack with disastrous results.

On another occasion a noise like a ball bearing buzz under the hood kept getting louder. My diagnosis consisted of loosening belts and turning the alternator pulley; it was nice and quiet. Next, the water pump; it, too, was quiet. The last possibility was the air conditioner idler pulley or compressor. The idler pulley was the way of adjusting the air conditioning belt. There is a bearing inside that pulley; turning the pulley by hand had a rough feel and made a grating sound. Removing and disassembling the bracket to remove the bearing was a fairly simple matter of removing nuts and bolts, then taking the bearing to an auto parts store to match up a new replacement. Reassembling and adjusting the belt correctly took care of the noise.

While taking a weekend trip in this car I heard a loud clanking noise under the hood. The noise lasted only a few seconds, and the car kept running properly, but the air conditioner immediately stopped cooling. At the time I was traveling on "Alligator Alley," the two-lane road through the Everglades between the Atlantic Ocean and the Gulf of Mexico. There were no other cars around so I stopped as soon as I could and opened the hood. The idler pulley bracket, containing the pulley and bearing, had come apart where it had been welded.

I did not start walking back to look for the part that fell off as I really did not want an alligator to spot me walking and decide to have me for lunch. Also, I did not know if the broken part had landed on the road or had bounced off the road and landed in the swamp, which came up to the edge of the narrow road. I stood by the car and looked back but did not see the part. The road was barely wide enough for two trucks to pass in opposite directions, and there was no place wide enough to turn around.

The air conditioner belt was ruined, and I was able to remove it so it would not get tangled in the engine fan and cause real damage. I was able to continue on my way using nature's "seventy plus four" air conditioner (i.e., seventy miles an hour with all four windows rolled down)!

It took a while for me to locate another bracket. Since this was an aftermarket hang-on unit, the bracket was not made by Chrysler and thus not available through a Chrysler dealer. After much junkyard shopping I finally located a bracket I could make work. After I installed the bracket and a new belt, the air conditioner cooled again.

Eventually rust began to show along the bottom of the doors and also around the rear glass plus a few other places. I was able to borrow a sandblaster (and the right kind of fine sand) as well as a grinder. I got rid of all the rust and immediately covered the bare metal with fiberglass material and the "bondo" material to smooth out the patch, then primed them. I was able to get the car professionally painted at a very fair price. Since the upholstery, dashboard and everything else inside was green I decided to have the outside painted green. Before the actual paint job I had access to spray equipment so I painted the door jambs and inside the doors and trunk and under the hood so the car would look as though it had always been light green. The professional job on the outside of the car turned out beautifully.

Unfortunately, about eighteen months later, rust started to form again — just a little at first, then gradually worse until it was just about as bad as when I fixed it. I did not fix it again.

After I had owned this car for seven or eight years a sudden overheating problem developed. It was a frustrating problem as no leaks were apparent and the thermostat and hoses checked okay. Finally, the problem was located. The impeller had come apart inside the water pump. Not only was it not pumping, but the pieces of the impeller actually restricted the flow of water through the pump. Replacing the pump immediately corrected the problem. Usually these pumps go bad by leaking; it is quite unusual for this problem to occur.

Altogether I drove this car more than 90,000 miles, the most I had ever driven one car. Though it had only 27,000 on it when I bought it, the car had 120,000 miles on it by the spring of 1981, after I had owned it for ten years.

Rust was again taking its toll. The transmission was getting spongy and would not always shift. Replacing the filter and using Ford fluid helped considerably. By the spring of 1981 it was a spare car and I knew the end was approaching. One Sunday afternoon when I was driving home after running an errand, I suddenly heard the loud rap of a con-

The connecting rod removed from the 1967 Valiant's number two cylinder after the bottom of it came off and caused the engine to lock up. This connecting rod now serves the author as a paperweight.

necting rod knock. I immediately shut off the ignition and coasted into a parking lot and pushed it into an empty space.

The next morning I had the car towed to where I could work on it. I tried to turn the engine over, but it was stuck. After removing all the usable parts prior to calling a junkyard I decided to see what had happened. I removed the cylinder head and found three pistons at top dead center. No more than two at a time can be at top dead center under normal conditions.

Then I was able to pry the flywheel teeth through the hole where the starter had been before I removed it. The rod cap had come off the number two connecting rod, and the top portion had become wedged between the crankshaft and the bottom of the cylinder block and was beaten to about a forty-five-degree angle. I was able to pull the piston and rod assembly out through the top of the cylinder bore. When I first heard the knock I probably could have stepped down hard on the gas and had the connecting rod come through the side of the block, but I didn't want to do that. I removed the piston and wrist pin from the connecting rod, and it now serves me as a paperweight.

This was the first car I owned that had what the U.S. auto industry called its dual braking system. Until that time there was a master cylinder with one reservoir chamber holding the brake fluid. A hose and pipe arrangement went to each individual wheel cylinder. Under normal conditions that was sufficient. However, if a leak developed in any one of the hoses or pipes or one of the wheel cylinders, all the fluid in the reservoir would leak out, and the brake pedal would immediately go all the way to the floor. The driver then had no way to stop the car using the foot brakes. With the new system, the master cylinder had two reservoir chambers, one for the front brakes and one for the rear brakes. Now, a leak would render only two of the wheels without brakes. The two remaining brakes could stop the car, providing it was not an emergency stop. Although only brakes for either front or rear worked, it was better than no brakes at all. Eventually, the system was modified somewhat by having diagonally opposite brakes connected to the same reservoirs chamber, so the right front and left rear were on the same system, and the left front and right rear were on the other.

When all U.S. car makers converted from the clutch and brake pedals protruding through the floor to hanging down from the dashboard for the 1955 models, master cylinders were moved from under the floor, below the driver's feet, to under the hood. That made checking the unit for fluid much easier. Replacement was much easier as well because bleeding the unit was usually not necessary.

With the master cylinder under the floor it was necessary to jack up the car to disconnect the pipes from the master cylinder. Since they were on the same plane, just about level with each other, some fluid would leak out when the pipes were disconnected. When the cylinder was replaced some air would be trapped in each pipe when connected to the new master cylinder. The procedure was to bleed the air from each pipe at the wheel farthest from the master cylinder, which would be the right rear, then the left rear, then the right front and finally the left front, which was closest to the master cylinder.

Beginning with the 1955 models with the master cylinder under the hood, up higher, the fluid would not leak out of the pipes to the wheel cylinders. The new master cylinder had to be bled to remove air from it, but this could be done easily from under the hood.

The procedure was basically to remove the old master cylinder slowly and carefully so that the pipes could not move around, jiggle or vibrate. The next step was to fill the reservoir with brake fluid before installing it. Then one connected the pipes to the new master cylinder only about three threads and finished installing the master cylinder properly and securely and to its bolts on the dashboard and to the pedal connection. Then, with the pipe fittings still loose, one slowly pushed the brake pedal down *once.* Then one filled the reservoir again and, with the pipe fittings still loose, *slowly* pushed the brake pedal down *once* again. Finally one tightened the pipe fittings all the way tight and filled the master cylinder reservoir again. Now the system would be free from air, and the brake pedal would feel solid when pressed. A rag or two under the old master cylinder before removal would have caught the brake fluid lost during the bleeding procedure. This procedure was the same for both the single reservoir type from 1955 through 1966 or the dual type from the 1967 and later models.

After I had owned this car about three years a rather unusual problem developed, unusual to me at least. I smelled gasoline sometimes while driving; it seemed to come and go. The first thing I did was to look under the hood. No leaks were obvious, but to be on the safe side I replaced the fuel filter and its hoses. No change. I then looked under the rear of the car around the gas tank and its connections. No sign of any leak there. The car's gas mileage had not dropped enough to be noticed. Finally, I took it to a mechanic I knew who had a lift and who I knew I could trust. I told him what I had already done and where I had looked.

As soon as he put the car up on the lift he found the problem. Since the fuel pump was on the right side of the engine, the steel gasoline pipe ran from the gas tank along the right side of the car's frame. For reasons I have never figured out, the steel pipe had rusted through where the pipe went under the area of the right front door. Although just a pin hole, it left a gasoline stain all along the pipe and surrounding area that was easily spotted from underneath.

The mechanic loosened the clamps enough to pull the line away from the frame far enough to cut out the rusted section. Then he cut off a section of regular fuel line hose from his roll, about a foot longer than the steel section he had removed. He overlapped each end about six inches to allow for vibration, then put a hose clamp on each end and reinstalled the pipe into its clips. That was the one and only time I had such a problem on any of my cars. The repair held as long as I had that car.

31 • *1962 Dodge*

In the autumn of 1971 I had only one car, the recently purchased 1967 Valiant (#30). I located a 1962 Dodge Dart four-door sedan with automatic transmission and no other accessories, not even a heater, defroster or air conditioning. Since it was to be a spare car, I decided to tolerate it with no heater or air conditioning.

During the late 1950s through 1962, the Dart was a full size car. Chrysler did a bit of dealer model shuffling for its 1961 model year when it dropped the DeSoto line of cars. Prior to that time, Dodge, De-Soto and Chrysler dealers all carried Plymouth as well. Chrysler decided to give the low-priced Plymouth line to Chrysler dealers only and to make comparable cars for Dodge dealers. For 1961 Dodge was given the Valiant-like Dodge Lancer. Both Valiant and Lancer were very successful.

In 1960 car drivers saw the introduction of the Valiant from Chrysler, the Ford Falcon and the Chevrolet Corvair, all compacts. All were very successful as the American public wanted a U.S.-built small or compact car. Dodge had used the word "Lancer" on some of its fancy models, so Dart and Lancer were familiar names for Dodge.

For 1963 the Lancer compact line was dropped by Dodge, and the compact Valiant look-alike car was given the name Dart. For the first time Dart became a compact. This 1962 Dart of mine was the last of the full size cars with the name Dart. The Dodge Lancer compact was made during the 1961 and 1962 models only. Only Valiant was made as a 1960 model.

When I found this car on a used car lot it had a terrible vibration. I presumed it was a broken rear engine mount; I played the vibration bit for all it was worth and got the car for not much more than junk

The author's 1962 Dodge Dart; the car did not have a heater or defroster. It is now illegal to build a car that way.

price. On the way home from buying it I stopped at an auto parts store and bought a rear mount. Replacing it was a simple matter of removing four bolts, raising the rear of the engine slightly, removing the broken mount, installing the new one, reinstalling the bolts and lowering the rear of the engine to normal and tightening the bolts—altogether about a twenty-minute job. I was right as the vibration was gone as soon as I replaced the rear mount.

Although this car was dent free, with only minor rust, it was not exactly a cream puff. The original white paint was thin. Whenever rust would begin to show through the trunk lid I would use some rubbing compound on the paint. This removed the rust and brought a slight shine back to the paint for a couple of months. The door upholstery was less than perfect, although usable. The front seat already had an aftermarket seat cover which looked fairly new.

This car had one idiosyncrasy I never bothered to get fixed. It would not hold in park. I presumed that the parking pawl was broken inside the transmission, but since it was probably resting in the bottom of the transmission somewhere and since the foot-operated parking brake held the car, I did nothing about having it fixed. The object of this car was to avoid spending any more money on it than absolutely necessary to keep it running safely.

Once while driving this car the engine began to miss, like a burned valve. When I removed the valve cover I saw that some rocker arms had moved frontward and backward on the rocker arm shaft, causing them not to come in contact with the particular valves. I learned that a rebuilt rocker arm shaft assembly was cheaper to buy than the individual parts. Replacing required removing and replacing a few bolts, plus getting all the push rods lined up properly. With that done, the car ran properly again.

Another time, when I started the engine I heard a cracking noise under the hood for a few seconds. This happened only when the car had been standing overnight or for a very long time. It gradually took longer and longer for the noise to stop. Eventually I realized that this was an exhaust leak, a cracked exhaust manifold. When the engine started, the first thing to get hot was the exhaust manifold, so the heat made it expand and seal the crack. As the engine was started more often, the crack spread and stayed loud for a longer time. I found a used manifold; replacing it was a routine matter of soaking all the nuts and bolts involved with penetrating oil, then removing them. Reinstalling the new manifold is a little tricky. Although basically it is just reinstalling the nuts and bolts, care must be taken to tighten them in the correct sequence and not to overtighten, not much more than finger tight. The whole job took about three hours.

On a different occasion while driving this car in a 40-mph zone in normal traffic, I stepped down on the gas pedal, and the engine returned to idle. I managed to limp into a bank parking lot where I discovered a broken accelerator cable. When I eventually found a replacement, the problem was easily solved in about fifteen minutes. Meanwhile, after setting the idle a little faster I limped home at about 15 mph. Although this car was a little over ten years old at the time, none of the Dodge or Plymouth dealers for miles around had one of these in stock, and I wound up having to get a used one from a junkyard.

Although the 1962 big Dodge and Plymouth models would have to be high on the all-time list of the ugliest cars made in this country, they were usually very dependable. So I was quite surprised when I lent this car to someone who said they could not use it because it would not stay running, which was very unlike this car. When I had parked it earlier in the day it was running fine. The description was that the engine would stall as soon as it started. I suspected the ballast resister for the ignition system had gone bad and confirmed this by connecting a jumper wire across the resistor, then starting the engine. It ran beautifully as usual. The friend got mad at himself for not having thought of this. Replacing the ballast resistor was very quick as it is under the hood on the firewall held in place by two bolts. Since this was an electrical item it could go bad at any time, just like a light bulb burning out. I am glad I was at home when it happened.

As this car was approaching 145,000 miles after my having owned it about four years (where I had to drive it twenty interstate miles to work every day and another twenty miles back home), I was wondering how many miles I could get from it. One morning I noticed that the heat gauge was showing hot. I managed to get off the interstate and add water at a gas station. It took very little water and had not overheated before. These slant six automatics were well known for their cool running. I looked for signs of leaking or overheating but didn't see any. The engine was still running warmer than usual. As I approached my exit ramp and took my foot off the gas pedal, I heard a pop noise, and the engine stopped running. I knew that there was plenty of gasoline in the tank.

After I coasted out of the way and stopped I tried to start the engine. It spun over effortlessly, with no resistance, exactly like the 1923 Lincoln (#6) had done when its timing chain had jumped, over twenty-five years earlier. To verify my suspicion I removed the air cleaner and held one hand over the top of the carburetor while working the starter solenoid from under the hood; there was no suction at all. This verified my jumped timing chain theory. I was able to get someone from work to pull me into the parking lot where I was headed; there I removed the usable parts and called a junkyard.

Even though this car was not trouble free, it served me well for what I paid for it and how many miles it had and how long I was able to use it. Replacing the timing chain and gears is not an impossible job, and had the car been younger with fewer miles, I would have fixed it myself.

Most Chrysler products of this era had the push buttons for the transmission located on the left side of the dashboard within easy reach of the driver's left hand. The push button panel was almost completely vertical with a handle in a slot to put the transmission into park. This was one of the few Chrysler-built models to have the push buttons and parking handle horizontally on the dashboard's lower edge, to the right of the steering column. The parking handle slid right to left instead of up and down as on the other system. The horizontal system worked just as well as the vertical systems.

After I had owned this car about three years the right front engine mount broke. This was not the same one I had replaced when I first bought the car. I bought a new mount at an auto parts store near where I worked. The following Saturday I replaced it. It was a matter of jacking the engine up slightly, removing nuts and bolts and the broken mount, then reversing the process to install the new one. It was a simple but rather dirty job. The only problem was that two weeks later the new mount broke, and I had to do the job over again. The same parts store sold me another one and promised me a full refund as soon as I brought the broken one back. The store was as good as its word on the refund. The only problem was that two weeks later it broke again. Rather than spending every other Saturday replacing engine mounts, I went to a different parts store that had a reputation of selling higher-quality parts. That one lasted as long as I had the car, about another three years. That was the only car to ever give me motor mount problems of any kind.

32 · 1962 Buick

A couple of months before the 1962 Dodge Dart (#31) expired a friend of a friend, who had a 1962 Buick LeSabre convertible, passed away. He was up in years, and the only possessions he had were his clothing and this car. He had no family and had given my friend power of attorney to settle his affairs. The car was rough, and my friend had no use for it. He knew I needed to replace the car I had just junked and that I was low on cash at the moment. He said that he would give me the car provided I would get the title and license plate put in my name and get liability insurance before actually taking the car. I had planned to do all those things anyway, and as soon as I showed him I had done those things, the car was mine. Certain Buick historians say that Buick did not make a convertible in the LeSabre series in 1962. Apparently their information is incorrect because I had one!

There actually was a Mr. Buick. He came from Scotland with his parents as a young child in the mid-1850s. The decorations on the hood and other ornaments of modern Buicks are adaptations of the Buik family coat of arms from Scotland ("Buik" is the old Scottish spelling).

Buick found himself in the plumbing supply business in the 1880s and 1890s, when most plumbing was outside. One of several patents he had was the application of porcelain to steel and cast iron. This made it possible to get items such as wash stands, sinks, bath tubs, and toilet fixtures clean and therefore sanitary to the point where they could be brought inside the house. Buick make a lot of money with this invention as it changed the way the world lived.

Early in the twentieth century Buick sold the plumbing supply business and patents in order to go into the automobile business. He went through all his money quickly, and by 1903 he was secretary of

The author's 1962 Buick LeSabre convertible. Some Buick historians believe that a convertible was not made in the LeSabre series for the 1962 model, but here is one!

the company bearing his name. A carriage maker, William C. Durant, was encouraged to take over, and he managed to turn the company around. The business was too fast paced for Buick, so he left in 1907.

Durant used Buick as the basis for founding General Motors very secretly in 1908. All three Chevrolet brothers, Louis, Gaston and Arthur, worked for Buick at one time or another. Walter P. Chrysler got his start in the automobile business working for the Buick division of General Motors, and so did Charles W. Nash. Buick was not successful on his own; on March 5, 1929, he died broke and forgotten over twenty years after leaving the Buick Motor Company.

This car looked like it had all of its original paint as none of its dents had been painted over. It had fairly good white sidewall tires. The air conditioner looked like it had not worked for a long time, probably due to a leaking evaporator core. The original black top was in the raised position. I tried to put it down once, but it would not go down; I did not try again.

I had this car only a few months as it was not dependable. Sometimes the starter would engage and sometimes not. The last straw came when I heard the unmistakable sound of a front wheel bearing coming apart. I was close to home when this happened, and I continued on home very slowly and parked it. I knew that the bearing might come completely apart while driving and lock up, causing disastrous results.

The following Sunday afternoon I slowly drove to a junkyard about five miles away. It turned out that I arrived when the yard was closed. It was located on a four-lane, divided highway. As I turned left to pull into the junkyard driveway I felt the front wheel bearing break completely and collapse just as I was in the median strip. The wheel locked up and would no longer roll. I had no choice but to leave the car there after removing my license plate. The next day I signed over the title and mailed it to the junkyard. The next time I passed that junkyard I saw the car inside the fence and the wheel and brake drum removed where I had heard the bearing break apart.

33 · *1967 Plymouth*

My next purchase was another 1967 Valiant. It, too, was a slant six automatic, four-door sedan; this one had factory air conditioning and power steering. It was the fanciest Valiant made that year, the Signet. The first 1967 Valiant was the medium series V-200.

Chrysler made big model changes for the 1967 Plymouth Valiant and Dodge Dart. The same basic chassis was retained although many components were improved, modernized and upgraded. The appearance was altogether new. The new body and chassis were so popular that they were retained, almost unchanged, for ten years until replaced by the Plymouth Volare and Dodge Aspen models in 1976. The biggest changes were made to accommodate the new-style bumpers for the 1973 and later models. Each year some fairly minor facelift-type changes were made to grille work, parking lights, taillights, and so on.

I found this car, too, on a used car lot. The only problems with the car when I bought it were that a rear wheel cylinder would not release completely and there was no key to the trunk. Having already junked a couple of cars like this I knew I had a trunk lock cylinder with keys. All I had to do was to remove the rear seat to open the trunk from the inside, then replace the lock cylinder with one to which I already had keys. The rear wheel cylinder overhaul and a new drum and brake shoes took care of that problem. Replacing the shoes on the other rear wheel prevented any chance of uneven braking.

Both 1967 Valiants were white when I bought them. Late in 1973 I had a chance to have the first one painted professionally at a very reasonable price. Since the upholstery was green, I had the car painted light green. Eventually I had the second Valiant painted as well; since the inside was blue I had it painted light blue.

The author's two 1967 Valiants. The one on the left, with bumper guards, is #33; the second one is #30.

This car was very dependable, so once when I had to take an airplane trip I drove this car to the airport and left it in the long-term (two weeks) parking lot. The only tools I brought with me in the car were a pair of jumper cables. When I put them in the trunk I wondered why I was doing it. After returning from the trip and placing the luggage in the trunk, I went to start the engine to drive home. Nothing, flat. Then I remembered the jumper cables.

The parking lot was arranged so that cars pulled in facing each other with the front bumpers almost touching. I noticed that the car in front of mine was a medium-priced Pontiac with an outside hood release. I opened the hood of my car and also the Pontiac's and noted that the cables were long enough to reach both batteries. As soon as I attached the last cable the dome light came on in my car. I immediately twisted the headlight knob and it went off. Since it had been daylight when I parked two weeks earlier I did not notice the light being on.

I waited about five minutes with jumper cables connected before trying to start my car. It started right up and ran fine. I removed the jumper cables, closed the Pontiac's hood, closed my hood, placed the jumper cables back in the trunk, said a thank you prayer, and thanked the Pontiac owner in absentia. By the time I arrived home about forty-five minutes later the alternator had brought the battery back up to normal. A few days later, when I was certain there was no battery or alternator problem, I put the jumper cables away.

After I had owned this car about a year the air conditioner stopped cooling. A trip to a mechanic was all it took to determine that the expansion valve, or "H" valve, was stuck. Replacing it and the drier and freon made things cool again.

About a year after the A/C problem came a cracked exhaust manifold, just like on the 1962 Dodge Dart (#31). As before, it was just a matter of getting a used manifold, then removing the cracked one and replacing it with the good one to get things quiet again.

Another problem unique to this car was a sudden drop in oil pressure; the red dashboard light came on very bright. I immediately shut the engine off and checked the oil; it was full. The most likely problem was the oil pump. I was hesitant to keep driving the car with the oil light on before I could replace the oil pump over the weekend, so I took it to the same mechanic who had replaced the air conditioner expansion valve near where I worked. I drove those five miles very slowly, not allowing the engine to go above fast idle. Replacing the oil pump was the solution as the oil light went out, and no apparent engine damage resulted.

This car lasted about three years. One night on the way home, at about 135,000 miles, I heard a pounding noise from the engine. It was not a connecting rod knock; I presumed that it was a main bearing. I managed to get the car to the side of the road just as the engine locked up, never to turn over again. The next day I was able to remove the parts I wanted to keep, then I called a junkyard.

34 · *1964 Ford*

In January 1979 I found a 1964 Ford Fairlane four-door sedan with the six-cylinder engine and automatic transmission. It also had a hang-on air conditioner which blew ice cube cold. At the time this car was built the Fairlane was a medium-size car, not the large car the Fairlane had been a few years earlier. As many people know, the name Fairlane was taken from the name Fair Lane (two words), which Henry Ford had given to the estate he built in 1919 and in which he died in 1947.

The 1962–1964 Fords were all quite similar in appearance, having had mainly facelift style changes from one year to the next. In my opinion, the 1964 models were the nicest looking.

The Mustang was introduced in 1964 as a 1965 model. The six-cylinder Mustang was built on the Falcon chassis, and the V-8 Mustang was built on the Fairlane V-8 chassis. I prefer the straight six-cylinder engine and think that they have the right amount of power, are reasonably simple in construction and are easy to maintain. Except for the Mustang, Ford made tremendous changes for its 1965 models, and I personally think the 1964s were much more attractive.

The body on this car was close to dent free and rust free, but the original paint was poor. This car drove very nicely, but after a few months the front brakes went bad. Replacing the shoes, turning the drums and rebuilding the wheel cylinders took care of that problem.

Then a more expensive problem developed: Sometimes the transmission would not shift out of low gear. The linkage checked okay. One possible diagnosis was that the external solenoid had gone bad. Replacing it myself did not help. The only other possible diagnosis was that the internal clutches and maybe other things inside the transmission were at fault. Since replacing or rebuilding the transmission would

The author's 1964 Ford Fairlane. At this time the Fairlane was no longer the large-size Ford.

cost more than I had paid for the car, I decided to drive it as long as I could.

The problem was getting worse, and it was taking longer to shift out of low gear. My letting up on the accelerator to coax it to shift was working less and less often. I had already begun to take only backroads to stay off main highways in low gear. I had even resorted to going fairly fast in low gear and then shifting into neutral and coasting when traffic permitted. That was not a smart way to drive, and I knew I could not keep on doing that.

It broke my heart to drive that car to the junkyard with ice cube cold air and new front brakes, but that is eventually what I had to do. I had the car about eight months.

This car also had a dark film on all of its windows to keep out a lot of the sun's rays. It was probably illegal to have it so dark. Although of course wanting to keep everything legal, I mainly did not like the overall appearance it gave the car. Removing the film required many hours of scraping with a tool containing a single-edge razor blade. The effort was well worth it, as the car seemed to take on a new, bright, cheerful appearance when the windows were clear and clean.

35 · *1971 Chevrolet*

In about June 1979 I was able to buy a 1971 Chevrolet Bel Air four-door hardtop. The 1971 Chevrolet "big cars" (e.g., Bel Air and Impala) had been modernized from the 1969–1970 models which were almost identical. The 1972–1974 big cars were facelifted carryovers from the 1971 models, the biggest change being made to accommodate new bumper systems. I had gotten a bad taste in my mouth for Chevrolets due, in large part, to my #1 car, the 1929 Chevrolet. The only other Chevrolet I had owned was the 1942 blackout (#7), which I didn't have very long due to unforeseen circumstances.

The only reason I bought this car was that it was available when I needed it at a very low price I could handle. I could not see myself growing old with it, but I hoped it would fulfill my needs at the moment. Had the price not been as low as it was I would not have bought it.

This car had a V-8 engine, and ice cube cold air conditioning, excellent tires but only a two-speed automatic transmission. It also had rust under the vinyl top and some bumps and dents. I did not like the four-door, hardtop style as it lent itself to squeaks and rattles. This one was no exception: It squeaked and rattled. Early on, the starter went bad so I bought a rebuilt one.

The vinyl top had been added on, not factory installed, meaning that it was more prone to form rust on the metal underneath the vinyl. I knew this when I bought the car, but, since the price was very low, I bought it anyway. I took a utility knife and a gallon of enamel reducer and proceeded to remove the vinyl top. The knife cut the top, and the enamel reducer dissolved the glue adhesive. The rust turned out to be a little worse than I had expected but still repairable.

The author's 1971 Chevrolet.

Although this car started quickly (after I replaced the starter) and ran well for what it was, I could just never get to like it well for reasons I can't really explain.

I knew a fellow who knew exactly what shape the car was in and was aware that I really didn't like the car and could not get enthusiastic about it. He made me an offer of about what I had in the car; I took it and got out from under the car after about six months.

36 · *1969 Dodge*

In early 1980 I was able to buy a 1969 Dodge Dart slant six, automatic, four-door sedan with power steering and brakes and factory air conditioning for wholesale price. This was a compact car, the same size as the Plymouth Valiant. About this time my first 1967 Valiant (#30) was starting to get tired. I had had that 1967 Valiant for eight years and would have it two more years.

The body of the 1969 Dart was dent free, and the paint would shine if enough elbow grease were applied to it with polish and wax. I was to have this 1969 Dart more than five years. Except for normal items I would expect to replace, this car was almost trouble free. The only real problem was a power steering leak, one place at the seal in the pump gear box and another in the pump. Neither was a breakdown; I just kept adding fluid until I could get them both fixed at the same time.

Once at an old car show and flea market there was a fellow with water pumps, nothing but water pumps, all-new old stock. He did not know what most of them fit, and he had a price of $5.00 each on them. I recognized the one for the slant six Chrysler engine, so I gladly paid $5.00 for it although I did not need it at the time. Normal price was $35.00 to $40.00 at the time. The next time I was in an auto parts store I bought gaskets for it. I put these away for future reference and eventually used them.

Another time I was in a discount store that was eliminating its inventory of auto parts at cost prices. I found two new voltage regulators. Again, I did not need one at the time but, since I was able to get them so cheaply, I bought them both. I eventually used them.

A couple of times the air conditioner stopped cooling. Each time the problem was the expansion valve ("H" valve); a new drier is also

The author's 1969 Dodge Dart.

required when the freon system is opened up to completely correct the problem.

This car began wearing out all at the same time. In mid-1985 I was on my way to an old car show about 50 miles from home. For close to a year the rear wheel bearing noise had been getting worse. Also the sponginess in the transmission did not improve after replacing the filter and fluid. While I was driving to the car show the engine began to overheat, then locked up. I was out in the country so I waited about an hour; then the engine was cool enough to restart.

It would barely run and was now smoking badly. By now I had given up plans to make the car show and had started back home. Continuing to add water did not stop the overheating, and it quit running again, this time for good; I was able to coast off the road.

A state highway patrol trooper stopped and checked things, then gave me a ride to the nearest town where there was a Greyhound bus station. I had to wait only about an hour to get my a bus to take me within a mile of home. I then got into my other car (#39) and drove back to the scene of the breakdown, where I removed my brand-new battery, my license plate, and a few other items. On Monday morning I called a fellow I knew who lived in the area and told him about the car. I asked him to call a junkyard for me and take whatever he could get for it and buy a round of soft drinks for himself and friends with what he got for it. I signed the title and had it notarized and mailed it to him.

37 · *1969 Pontiac*

This was a 1969 Pontiac Catalina two-door hardtop I acquired in 1981. The Pontiac name was given to this brand of cars because it was built in Pontiac, Michigan, which was in Oakland County. General Motors bought the Oakland Motor Car Company in 1909 and used the Oakland as a high-priced car. GM also purchased the Northway Engine Company from Robert Northway and had Northway build engines for Oldsmobile and Oakland during the 1910s and into the 1920s. Unfortunately, those Northway engines had design flaws. In the mid-1920s GM decided to give Oakland a lower-priced car, Pontiac.

In 1969 the Catalina was one of the large series of the Pontiac name. It came with a large V-8 engine. Being a big, heavy car it was not known for excellent gasoline mileage but was built for comfort and prestige. All of them came with GM's automatic transmission as standard equipment.

The original owner had bought this car as a demonstrator in 1969. He was not known to take excellent care of his cars. It still had all the dents it had acquired over the past twelve years, and, where the paint was not too faded to see, it was original. The expensive Catalinas came with power steering and brakes as standard equipment. This car also had factory air conditioning, but it had stopped working several years earlier because the owner would not spend the money to have it fixed. The repair would have involved a new evaporator, compressor, and all that goes with them and amounted to several hundred dollars at the time. He knew that I needed a car; in addition, his wife was getting after him to do something with the car because it looked so bad. He let me have it for a very friendly price.

I did not like a two-door car because the doors are so big (long),

The author's 1969 Pontiac Catalina two-door hardtop. This car came from the original owner, who bought it as a demonstrator in 1969.

especially on a big car like a Pontiac Catalina. This is not a car I would have purchased if I had had the luxury of being able to shop at leisure. But I needed a car in fairly good running order at a low price. My friend also had the satisfaction of knowing that the car was going to someone who would not abuse it. His wife had the satisfaction of getting rid of the eyesore in the driveway.

The owner told me that while on vacation a couple of years earlier something had happened with the engine's valve train on the right bank. He had had to stop at an out-of-town garage and had been at the mercy of that garage owner to fix the car properly. The garage had repaired it as cheaply as possible at a fair price, but after I had the car for close to a year the noise returned. I knew that it would be expensive to fix so I did nothing about it.

Eventually, a miss developed in that cylinder and became worse. Since the car was not worth the price of the repair I did not have it fixed. I just kept on driving the car as it got worse. Then one day at home, it refused to start, making a noise every time that valve moved on that particular cylinder. I made no attempt to repair the problem or to even determine exactly what it was. I merely removed the few useable items from the car and called a junkyard.

38 · *1973 Pontiac*

Another fellow I knew had a 1973 Pontiac Catalina station wagon. It had been the expensive model with the wallpaper on the sides and power everything, including the tailgate that retracted into the floor and the back window that retracted into the roof. This was also a one-owner car whose owner took almost no care of it.

After ten years the engine had a miss, the A/C compressor was very noisy, the tailgate and the back window would not move either way, and every panel on the car was rusted through. The car looked and ran so poorly that the owner's wife refused to ride in it any more. I knew all this in the spring of 1983, when I had to junk the 1969 Pontiac (#37).

I asked the fellow how much he wanted for the car. He said that he did not want it on his conscience to ask anyone for money for that car. Since he knew I needed a car and could probably use some sweat equity to get the car running better, he gave it to me.

The quickest and cheapest thing to do for the engine miss was to replace all eight spark plugs. Seven of them had easy access, but one was not easy to remove. The right front wheel had to be removed to get access to the first one on the right bank. When I removed it I noticed that it was an A-C brand while the other seven were a different brand. Since the original owner did not know how to change spark plugs, I wondered if that were one of the original spark plugs, never having been replaced since it was so hard to reach and was now badly fouled. Replacing the spark plugs corrected the engine miss.

My next project was to get the tailgate to go down and the back glass to go up into the roof. I removed a trim panel and garnish moldings to expose the wiring harness to those units. By tinkering with

The author's 1973 Pontiac Catalina station wagon, from the original owner. When the owner's wife found out that I needed a car she insisted that her husband give it to me, as she and her husband knew that I could probably get it into decent running condition and be able to use it.

jumper wires, and so on I found that the glass was stuck in its position in its tracks because its motor was bad. By disconnecting the wiring to the glass the strain was taken off the tailgate, which retracted into the floor opening and back as it was supposed to do.

Eventually I was able to free up the back glass so it would move up and down by hand, but I never got it to work electrically as it was designed to do. This meant that I could not lock the car completely. The four doors and the tailgate would lock properly, but the back glass could be opened by anyone who would place the palms of his hands on the glass and slide it up into the roof.

Once that turned out to be a good thing for me as I had locked the doors with the keys in the ignition. I had to call on someone in an office and fortunately was parked in the lot in such a way that the people in the office I was to visit could not see the car. I realized what I had done as soon as I did it but took the chance that no one would see my keys, including house key, in the ignition. I did not want to be late for my appointment. After I completed my appointment I saw that my keys were still in the ignition. I slid up the back glass and very ungracefully climbed in, over the tailgate.

The mechanic friend who had replaced the power steering seals on the 1969 Dodge Dart (#31) had a used A/C compressor for this style

GM car. It was a core that he kept for an exchange unit for times when he needed a rebuilt GM compressor. It had a good, quiet front bearing. These were special bearings and quite expensive. He switched them, and I wound up with a good, quiet A/C; it had always cooled properly.

This car was huge and, with its 400 engine and 400 transmission, quite powerful but gave very low gas mileage. I could almost watch the needle on the gas gauge go down. That car would pass anything on the road except a gas station. The friend from whom I had purchased the 1969 Pontiac (#37) knew that I did not like this '73 Pontiac because it used so much gas. A friend of his parents, a lady, was up in years and now by herself in the world and had a 1971 AMC Hornet she had purchased new twelve years earlier. The lady had recently suffered a stroke and would no longer be able to drive. Thinking of me, my friend spoke up for the car so I got it. As soon as I was able to get it in driving condition I junked the 1973 Pontiac after removing the A/C compressor and sealing it for my friend.

39 · 1971 AMC

This AMC Hornet had not run for a couple of months before the original owner suffered a stroke and was no longer able to drive. The car was the lowest-priced, two-door sedan with a six cylinder inline engine, automatic transmission, power steering and brakes and factory A/C. It also had the Ziebart rustproofing. The title was signed over to me for nothing, about what the car was worth at the time.

There were two reasons the car had not run: Both the carburetor and the brakes were bad. The carburetor had somehow developed a hole in the float bowl at the bottom. Repairing it consisted of removing the carburetor, turning it upside down, putting a fiberglass patch over the hole and checking the float for proper level. To be on the safe side I also replaced the fuel filter and added a second filter in the fuel line.

The brakes did not work at all. Although the pedal went all the way to the floor, the car didn't even slow down. All the wheel cylinders were leaking, soaking the brake lining. In addition, the two front brake hoses and single rear flexible hose were leaking; in addition, the steel brake lines going from the center of the rear axle to each rear wheel cylinder were rusted through. Replacing all of these, plus turning the drums and packing the front wheel bearings, gave me perfect brakes.

After I had the car running properly I tried my hand at the air conditioner. It turned out that the evaporator was leaking. I located one at a dealer, but the parts manager insisted on full retail price for it and would not budge. I did not buy it.

The original owner lived just a few blocks from the beach with its salt air. After I started using the car almost daily, the muffler became noisy due to being rusted through. A trip to Midas for a new muffler

The author's 1971 AMC Hornet, from the original owner.

and tail pipe solved that problem. The tires were questionable and mis-matched. A trip to a recap plant for all four tires revealed that the spare was one of the original tires on the car. The plant had a way of look-ing up the numbers on the tire, and, sure enough, the odd-size spare was made in 1971. Naturally, I made sure I traded in that tire. I did not feel like buying new tires for that car. The plant found that a front rub-ber bushing at one of the lower control arm struts was worn, so they replaced it.

One summer evening I had to pick up someone at the airport about 35 interstate miles away. I knew I didn't have enough gas in the tank for the round trip so I stopped at a gas station I had not used before and filled the tank with "regular." What I actually got, however, was about half a tank of gasoline and half a tank of water. Just a few min-utes after leaving the station the engine started to buck and miss and kept getting worse.

When I met the person at the airport I mentioned that the car was acting up. It continued worse and worse until it finally stopped run-ning completely. I was able to coast off the interstate. In just a few min-utes a state highway patrol trooper stopped to see why we were there. It was now about 7:00 PM and would be dark in about another hour. The trooper could see that we were stranded and offered to take each of us home with the other person's baggage.

The next morning I called a friend in the area, explained the situation to him and asked him to just get someone to drain the gas tank and to add about ten gallons so I could easily make it home. It was ready the next day, so I took a Greyhound bus to where the car had been towed and drove it home with no further problems. I never went back to that gas station again.

Another problem, one of the most serious, was the rust. Although this car had been rust proofed when new, there were places where the rustproofing material could not be applied, such as the roof and inside the rear quarter panels and the upper body panel between the trunk lid and the back window. Where the rustproofing was applied (such as on the hood, fenders, and trunk lid), the metal was rust free.

One of the unlikely rust areas was the roof above the right door. Apparently no one ever rode with the original owner as she must have almost never opened the right side door. The result was that dirt, leaves and other debris had collected there, retained moisture and rusted through the metal. The driver's door was perfect because she had opened it often enough to let some air circulate to get things dry and not accumulate leaves and so forth. Apparently she had set her groceries on the front seat or else on the rear floor so she didn't open the right door. In addition, the left quarter panel from the left quarter window all the way down was also rusted away. One of the quarter panel braces was exposed and badly rusted, almost all the way through.

This car was dependable once the fuel and brake systems were repaired, the tires and exhaust systems replaced, and so on. It gave considerably better gas mileage than the two previous big V-8 Pontiacs (#37 and #38) of course. The Hornet was a light car, but on a couple of occasions I drove 500 miles on interstates in one day without problems. I had the car for several months before I realized that the top of the gas tank was also the bottom of the trunk.

I had this car for about two years. I finally woke up to the fact that if this car were ever in even a moderate accident it would collapse because (1) it was a small car, (2) even the structural parts of the body were rusted away and (3) a bump from the rear with the center-fill fuel tank and no trunk floor as such could spread fire under the car instantly. I leisurely looked for something larger. When I found a car I liked I junked this Hornet as I did not want it on my conscience that I had sold a car so badly rusted.

In the early 1950s the remaining five major independent U.S. auto makers (Kaiser, Packard, Studebaker, Nash and Hudson) were all having financial problems, mainly because they did not have enough money behind them for research and so on. Kaiser merged with Willys Jeep for a short time but could not make ends meet, and Kaiser folded while Jeep remained. Packard and Studebaker merged. The Packard name lasted until 1958, when it looked much like a Studebaker. Studebaker eventually moved to Canada, where it finally went under in 1966.

George Romney engineered the merger between Nash and Hudson into the American Motors Corporation. One of Hudson's models had been named "Hornet." AMC kept that name and placed it on the lowest-priced AMC model. The last car with a Hudson or a Nash name was the 1957, after which all became known as Rambler. AMC eventually acquired Jeep, which became its best-selling vehicle. The early 1980s saw AMC add a four wheel drive passenger car, the Eagle. In 1986 Chrysler took over AMC, primarily to get its Jeep line of vehicles, and phased out the Eagle and the other AMC names. My 1971 AMC Hornet was the lowest-priced car made by American Motors that year.

When American Motors Corporation was formed in the mid-1950s two oldtime independents, Nash and Hudson, came together. Hudson had been in the family of Roy D. Chapin and his son almost since its founding in 1909. The Hudson department store in Detroit put up most of the money to get the company going, so the car was named Hudson.

Hudson revolutionized the automobile business in the United States beginning in 1919, when it had the Fisher Body Corporation build very low-priced enclosed bodies with no fancy upholstery or fittings. This brought the price of enclosed sedans down low enough so that almost every family could afford one. The rest of the industry followed, and in just ten years the ratio of 10% enclosed cars and 90% open cars, touring cars and roadsters was reversed to 90% enclosed sedans and coupes and only 10% open cars, which was the ratio in 1929. In the late 1940s one of the best-selling Hudson models was Hornet.

Nash went through several major changes during its life. Thomas B. Jeffery had been making bicycles in Chicago, using the name "Rambler" during the 1880s and 1890s. He realized that the bicycle fad had just about peaked and that the next fad would be horseless carriages. He sold the bicycle company and moved a few miles up the shore of Lake Michigan from Chicago to Kenosha, Wisconsin, where the began producing the Rambler automobile in 1902.

Meanwhile, Charles W. Nash had been working in Flint, Michigan, for the Durant-Dort carriage Company, eventually becoming superintendent. When William C. Durant took over the floundering Buick Motor Company in 1904, he turned it around and made money. In October 1908 Durant secretly formed General Motors, then went on a buying spree, picking up Buick, Oldsmobile, Oakland, Cadillac, and a host of other small car companies and suppliers. By late 1910 General Motors was broke and had to go very deeply in debt.

Durant was ousted as GM's head but was allowed to stay on the board of directors. Durant suggested that Nash be made president of General Motors. Under Nash's leadership GM made many technical advances and was able to pay off its tremendous debt on time, in 1915. Meanwhile, the Jeffery Company was also prospering by selling its Rambler automobiles. When Thomas B. Jeffery died in 1910, his son took over the company and renamed the car, the Jeffery.

In 1915 Durant had bought up enough GM stock to be back in control. Nash resigned as president, bought the Jeffery Company and immediately changed the name of the cars, trucks, and the company itself to "Nash." In 1936 Nash merged with Kelvinator, an appliance manufacturer. When Nash retired in 1937, George Mason became the company's president. In 1950 Nash resurrected the name "Rambler" for its small car.

The merger of Hudson and Nash to form American Motors continued until 1986, when AMC was purchased by Chrysler primarily to acquire AMC's Jeep division, which, by that time, was the only division of American Motors making any money. As the twenty-first century began, Daimler of Germany took over Chrysler Corporation.

Another bit of irony stretched as far back as 1911, when Nash hired Walter P. Chrysler to replace him as head of GM's Buick division. Although both men eventually left General Motors and each formed his own car-manufacturing company, they remained friends. Neither could possibly have foreseen the future, when spinoffs of each of their companies would eventually merge and then be taken over by a foreign manufacturer.

40 · 1983 Dodge

In the spring of 1986 I found what I had been seeking. For several months I had been looking for something easy to get into and out of. All the regular cars I checked out were too difficult. The days of the really comfortable 1949 through 1952 Chrysler products that were easy to enter and exit were gone. I didn't really want a truck, so the only logical alternative was a sport utility or station wagon or something equally tall.

Sport utilities were new on the market at the time and therefore expensive. Since I didn't want anything foreign or anything from General Motors, my search was narrowed to either Ford or Dodge/Plymouth. What I found was a 1983 Dodge station wagon.

This car was built, titled, insured and licensed as a station wagon; some people call it a window van. It was the smallest full-size van Dodge made in 1983. In 1984 Chrysler brought out its minivan.

My Dodge had insulation, upholstery, carpeting, and other niceties of the passenger-car type. It had a slant six automatic, power steering and brakes, factory air conditioning, cruise control, the big one-piece back door, windows all around, tinted glass, side opening (not sliding) doors, and white sidewall tires, all factory installed.

The Dodge dealer where I found the car had sold it new and had its complete service history. The previous owner had had the expansion valve (or "H" valve) replaced in the air conditioner; the A/C worked fine when I bought the car, This car had been built in August 1982 and sold retail in December 1982. The only thing I really didn't like was the odometer reading of almost 70,000 miles. The service record showed that the transmission had been serviced at the suggested 35,000 miles, so I had it done again, now at 70,000, and again at 105,000.

The author's 1983 Dodge station wagon. This was built, titled, licensed and insured as an automobile, not a van, because it was equipped as a car would be.

Shortly after I bought the car I replaced all the belts, hoses and spark plugs. On the slant six engine the #1 spark plug is behind the alternator. On the previous slant six automatics I had owned, it was a simple matter to loosen the alternator, slip the belt off the pulley, let the alternator swing down out of the way, replace the #1 spark plug, and then reverse the procedure to reinstall the belt. The other five spark plugs had easy access.

After I had owned the car about a year the engine would miss once in a while. I checked the spark plug and distributor wires, and they were all tight. The miss began to happen more and more often. Since I did not have experience with computerized or electronic ignition, I took the car to the nearby Dodge dealer from whom I had purchased it. I knew one of the service writers there and knew he would see that the problem was fixed properly and that I would be treated fairly. The problem turned out to be a bad reluctor inside the distributor.

About eight months after the reluctor replacement the air conditioner gradually stopped cooling. It was expansion valve time again.

When the expansion valve is replaced the drier must also be replaced; actually, any time the freon system is opened up the drier should be replaced. The previous expansion valve, the one the previous owner had paid for in 1985, had lasted about three years. Then the one I had replaced also lasted a bit over three years as I had to have it replaced in 1991.

Once, I began to notice that the gas gauge would only register between half and three quarters full just a few days after filling the tank. The tank held thirty-six gallons, and I knew I had not driven that much. It got to the point where the gauge would not register above about half when the tank was full. I took the car to a mechanic who came well recommended. He tested the wiring and found that the gauge itself was okay; the tank unit was bad. I did not have the facilities to remove the tank in order to remove the tank unit. To save time I bought the tank unit from a Dodge dealer, who dropped the tank to replace it.

Another time, while coming back from an old car show and still about 400 miles from home, I made a rest stop at an interstate service plaza. When I went to start the engine to continue, the engine turned over very slowly, but it did start. The alternator was not charging. I opened the hood and found the belt in place and the wires connected properly. I left the interstate at the next exit, which led to a good-size town. I was able to get a garage to look at it while I waited. I had to buy a rebuilt alternator and a voltage regulator. The mechanic connected the charger to the battery while doing the other work. This was the only alternator problem I had as long as I owned the car.

The two-tone paint finish on this car was tan (beige) and dark brown with the wheels also tan. It also had wide, white sidewall tires and stainless steel wheel covers. My opinion is that the white sidewall tires stand out much better if they are on black rims; this also makes the wheel covers stand out more.

One of the first things I did to this car was to clean all the wheels inside and out and paint them black enamel. I knew that it would not be too long before I would be buying tires.

Goodyear was the only tire company making the wide, white sidewalls in the size I needed. About five years later, when tire replacement time arrived again, the Goodyear store where I had bought the first set had moved, so I went to a different store nearer to where I worked. I told the fellow there what I needed, we agreed on the price, and I left the car there and went on to work. Shortly after lunch the fellow I had left the car with called and said that the car needed upper ball joints. I felt that he was just trying to sell me something I did not need, so I said "no." About a year later, when idler arm replacement was due, that mechanic checked the entire front end and suspension, including all four ball joints, and the only thing needing replacement was the idler arm.

The two trumpet horns on that car were located behind the left parking light and directly under the battery. The left parking light assembly had to be removed to gain access to the bolts holding the horns in place. When they went bad I took them off, carried them to an auto parts store to match up, and then installed the new ones. About three or four months later they went bad again; same procedure, only this time I was not charged for the new ones. About three or four months later they went bad again; same procedure and I was given two more new horns, again at no charge to me. The next time they went bad, in another three or four months, I went to a different auto parts store where a better brand was stocked. That pair lasted as long as I kept the car.

Shortly after I bought the car I noticed that the battery box was rusted away on one end and the battery was just sort of hanging out in space. I found that a replacement kit with just the battery tray was available, so I bought one and replaced it. About four years later it had rusted through again, so I did the job once more. It was okay as long as I had the car.

After I had owned the car about five years it began to run a little hot. I had the radiator and engine back flushed and a new thermostat installed, but those did not help. Replacing the radiator on that van was quite tricky as the shop manual said that it must come out from the bottom. Rather than attempt that myself I took the car to a radiator shop for a new radiator, hoses and antifreeze. It was noticed that the water pump was starting to seep, so it was replaced at the same time. It takes only a few minutes to replace the water pump with the radiator and hoses already removed.

The next day, on my way home in the late afternoon, the heat gauge went all the way over to "hot." I pulled over and looked under the hood. The lower hose was touching the alternator pulley and had rubbed through. Also, the alternator belt was on the wrong pulley of the alternator. I was able to fill the radiator with water and made it to an auto parts store, where I bought a new lower hose and a new alternator belt and antifreeze. When I arrived home I let everything cool down, including myself, then replaced everything properly. I drove the car a couple of days to make sure it didn't overheat again and ruin the thermostat, then took the rubbed through hose and frayed belt and the receipt back to the radiator shop. The owner apologized and gave me the amount of the receipt plus another $10.00 for my trouble and said that he would have a talk with his mechanic.

In late 1992 I noticed that the car seemed to wander and require more correction of the steering to keep going straight. The culprit turned out to be the idler arm in the steering. By now, 100,000 miles were showing on the odometer. I did not have the tools to replace it, so I got a mechanic to do so. When I started driving the car then, I had to get used to the way it steered all over again so that I would not over-correct and wind up some place I didn't want to be.

None of the repairs I mentioned was major, and I learned to expect things to need attention as a car approaches 100,000 miles.

Not long after buying this car I discovered how to change the oil and filter without it being apparent what I was doing. I changed my own oil and filter because I wanted to use 20W50 oil, which was not available at most gas stations. I also wanted to use a higher-quality filter than gas stations had available.

On every Chrysler product slant six engine for over twenty years, the filter was located on the right side of the engine near the rear of it. This car was built high enough off the ground to get under it with a flat-style plastic drain pan and the drain plug wrench without jacking up the car. Then I placed a smaller drain pan next to the first one, directly under the filter. Then the screws and clips surrounding the engine cover were removed, allowing the engine cover to be lifted off. Then I used the oil filter tool, unscrewed the filter and dropped it straight down into the small drain pan without spilling anything. Next came cleaning the filter base plate on the engine, lubricating the seal on the bottom of the new filter and screwing it on hand tight. I always managed to have a flat-style, one-gallon plastic jug; an empty windshield washer fluid jug was ideal. By this time all the oil had drained from the oil pan, and another quick trip underneath pulled the drain pans out and reinstalled the drain plug.

The PCV valve on the top of the engine's valve cover could easily be pulled out of its rubber grommet, a funnel added and the new oil poured in. The flat-type plastic jug fit perfectly on the right front door's running board with the door open, and the plastic funnel placed in it allowed pouring the used oil in without spilling. One or two of the one-quart plastic jugs, which had contained the new oil, could be used to hold the used oil when the one-gallon jug became almost full.

Reinstalling the PCV valve and the engine cover inside completed the job. The hood was never opened and the car was never jacked up. Everything was done with only the right front door open. The driver's door was opened for about two minutes to remove the screws and clips on the left side of the engine cover, then opened again to reinstall them when the job was finished. Since every gas station is required to accept used oil from anyone who brings it in, legal disposal was not a problem.

An early trip to Midas gave me a complete brake overhaul, wheel cylinders and calipers, drums and rotors turned, and so on. In the eight years I owned this car Midas replaced the pads three times and the rear shoes twice. I had to pay only for the first set of each. After about six years the end of the tail pipe was rusting away. I went to Midas fully expecting to buy a new tail pipe. They said that all I really needed was a splice where it had rusted away and that the rest of the exhaust system was fine.

During the several vacation trips I made in this car it performed flawlessly at interstate speeds. The cruise control proved to be a great convenience.

Although this car was built on a truck chassis, it was built as a passenger car, titled, licensed, and insured as a station wagon. It was assembled in Canada to U.S. specifications because the only Chrysler assembly plant for full-size vans at the time was in Canada. It is now being built in U.S. assembly plants.

Dodge has been building this full-size van since the late 1960s, and the basic body style has not changed except for taillights, grille work and trim changes. It is now available only with a V-8 engine and as a work truck with no windows or inside trim behind the driver's seat, as well as a window van like mine, and many versions in between.

Index